YOUR ATTITUDE IS SHOWING

A Primer on Human Relations

Elwood N. Chapman
Chaffey College, Alta Loma, California

 SCIENCE RESEARCH ASSOCIATES, INC.
Chicago, Palo Alto, Toronto, Henley-on-Thames, Sydney

A Subsidiary of IBM

Contents

Case Problems

Preface

The first edition of *Your Attitude Is Showing* was published eight years ago. Since that time hundreds of teachers have selected it as their classroom text in a wide variety of educational institutions; it has been heavily purchased by both big and small business and governmental organizations as an important training tool for both the new and experienced employee; it has found its way into the personal libraries of those interested in the human problems found in the work environment. Today it is recognized as a basic primer in the field of business human relations.

Your Attitude Is Showing is a positive book. It has helped individuals of all ages and backgrounds play their human relations roles with greater understanding and sensitivity. It has been of special help, however, to the young person faced with the problem of bridging the gap between school life and the world of work, because it has prepared him to cope with the many human problems that were waiting for him. This explains why the book has been so popular with the student who is getting ready to climb over the academic wall.

I believe this new edition will be enthusiastically welcomed by teachers, students, management people, and employees alike, because it has been revised based upon research and consultation with those who have used the first edition extensively. It will, therefore, meet the contemporary needs of both the individual and the organization. Three of the many new features are: (1) a special chapter that explores the racial and sexual overtones of occupational relationships; (2) an added chapter that pinpoints the causes and career implications of employee absenteeism; and (3) fresh material that will help the worker better understand and work with the difficult supervisor.

As you read and study *Your Attitude Is Showing,* please keep in mind that those who become good at human relations find greater on-the-job happiness, contribute more to the success of their organizations, and, if they are so inclined, quickly set the stage for their first promotion into supervisory or managerial positions.

"After all, I'm just an amoeba."

Introduction

As we go about the business of living we are not always conscious that we show our mental attitudes to friends, relatives, teachers, management people, co-workers, and customers. So that you may become more aware of this (and have some fun, too), this book has been illustrated with little attitude pictures like the one above. Each has been drawn to resemble the amoeba—that microscopic, one-celled creature which is gray in color, constantly changing in size and shape, and often referred to as the lowest form of life.

It is hoped that the little amoeba will act as a reminder to you that no matter where you are or what you are doing, *Your Attitude Is Showing.*

Each of the drawings has been copyrighted by E.N. Chapman, 210 West 6th Street, Ontario, California, 91762, and reproduction without his permission is expressly prohibited.

"I've heard all that old stuff before."

You Can't Escape Human Relations

Most employees drastically underestimate the importance of human relations in building their careers.

They pass it off as nothing more than common sense.

They say it is something one handles intuitively.

They claim it is something you automatically take care of when it happens, so why worry about it in advance?

But what exactly is involved in human relations?

You would be justified in saying that part of human relations is being friendly, pleasant, courteous, adaptable, and sociable. It is smiling. It is keeping out of trouble with fellow workers. It is following the rules of simple etiquette. It is good taste. It is getting people to like you. But as important as these characteristics are to personal success, they are not

Some Have — some Have not

Care — don't care

enough. Human relations is much more than just getting people to like you.

Human relations is also knowing how to handle sticky problems when they arise. It is learning how to work with demanding and sometimes unfair supervisors. It is understanding the personality of others and of oneself. It is building sound working relationships in forced associations where things can get touchy. It is knowing how to restore a working relationship that has deteriorated. It is learning how to live with one's frustrations without hurting others. It is building and maintaining relationships in many directions, with many different kinds of people, whether they are easy to get along with or not.

In the world of work, human relations can be understood only when viewed as a background to productivity.

Productivity!

Ah, there is a word worth knowing about. Why? Because that word is the key to your future and the future of the organization you have joined. Every employee is expected to produce at a certain level, so it is obvious that human relations *alone* won't take you very far in building your career. It is only one side to any personal success story. The other side is performance. Good human relations is no substitute for work. An employer is never interested for long in an employee who has a great attitude but produces very little. Work schedules must be met. The job must be completed. Good human relations cannot camouflage a sloppy performance. All employees, both new and experienced, are measured first on the amount of work they turn out. Your employer will expect you to do your share of the work load, and, if you are interested in moving ahead, you will want to do more than your share.

But getting the work out is only one side of the coin. You must accomplish this work and still be sensitive to the needs of those who work with you. You must perform your work without trying to show up your fellow workers or antagonizing them. You must carry your full load in such a way that others will be encouraged to follow you rather than reject you.

So there you have it.

[handwritten margin notes: "Build too much into it." / "Need not be complicated." / "All common—"]

No matter how ambitious or capable you may be, you cannot become the kind of employee you want to be, or the kind of employee management wants you to be, without learning how to work effectively with people. It is career suicide for you to join an organization and ignore the people who work around you. No matter what your experiences or attitudes have been in the past, you can't escape human relations.

Does this mean that you should deliberately set out to play a game of human relations on your new job? The answer depends upon what you mean by "playing a game."

If you mean that you should play up to those who can do you the most good and pay little attention to others, the answer is no.

If you mean you should devise a master strategy that will give you the breaks at the expense of other people, the answer is no.

If, however, you mean that you should sincerely do everything you can to build strong, friendly, and honest working relationships with *all* the people you work with—fellow employees and supervisors as well—the answer is an unqualified yes.

Does this come as a shock?

If so, think about it. For working hard is not enough in our modern society. It may have been years ago, but it isn't today. You, as a new employee, have a definite human relations responsibility.

You can't ignore it.
You can't shake it off.
You can't postpone it.
From the moment you join an organization you assume two obligations: (1) to do a job—the *best* job you can do in the work assigned to you; (2) to get along with *all* people to the best of your ability. It is the right combination of these two factors that spells success.

Perhaps you will graduate from high school or a community college in a few months and your first full-time job will be with a large service company. Or maybe you will complete a four-year college or university with a degree in engineering or business administration and elect to join a large industrial corporation. Or, after leaving the military, you may become a salesman in a small retail establishment. Or, after working a number of years for another company, you may decide to switch and try to make the most of your fresh start. The possibilities are endless, but no matter what your personal conditions are now or what they may be in the future, your first full-time job will give you your big chance. It is too early to tell, but you may wish to have a lifelong career with the company you join.

There will be one nice thing about your first big job. Whether you start out as a stock boy in a department store or as a member of a research team for a government bureau, chances are good you will receive some training as you get started on the job. This is true because *you were not employed so much for what you already know as for what you can learn in the future.* You were employed for your potential, and the company that has employed you wants to help you reach that potential.

To be sure, if you are employed as a secretary, your skill at taking shorthand is important. If you are employed as an apprentice machinist, your mathematical ability is important. If you are a college graduate employed under a planned training program, your general background in business administration or marketing is important. It would be foolish to say that the skills or abilities that you possess are unimportant. They helped you win your present position and they will help you make progress.

But they are not enough.

In order to make your education and experience work for you properly, you must now become "human relations smart." You must develop different skills in a different setting. You must learn the skills and techniques of working with others.

Why?

Because your behavior has a direct bearing on the efficiency of others. Because your contribution will not always be an individual contribution; it will often be a group effort, and you will only be a part of the group. Because what you accomplish will be in direct proportion to how well you get along with the people who work with you, above you, or for you.

You may not want to have it this way, but that's the way it is.

You will be one of many employees. Almost everything you do will have an effect on other people. If the effect is good, these people will do a better job. If the effect is bad, they will be less productive. Your *personal* work effort will not be enough. You must conduct yourself in such a manner that those who work with you and near you will also be more effective.

Sounds like a large order, doesn't it? It is. It is so big, in fact, that it may be the most difficult job you will ever encounter. It may also be the most important.

Now let's take a closer look at this word *productivity*. Productivity is a million-dollar word in business, industry, and government today. This is true because every organization is operated either to make a profit or to reach a certain level of productivity.

Management has ways of measuring work productivity. If you are employed by a manufacturing company, for example, and performing a certain task, your productivity can be measured by the amount of work you do. Some organizations employ time-study men to measure the time required to perform a given task, and to evaluate methods and establish standards of performance. You will be expected to exceed this standard. If you are employed in a sales organization, you may be given a sales quota that you are expected to reach or exceed.

The important point is that everyone's productivity is measured. We must all live up to the standards that prevail in our particular business. Some jobs are more easily measured than others; but there is some form of measurement or evaluation for every job.

However, our value is measured not only by the actual *work* we do, but also by the *contribution* we make to the department as a whole. This is human relations—as management sees it. Productivity is not only an individual matter; it is also a divisional or departmental matter. For management has discovered that the way in which people get along together has a great deal to do with departmental productivity.

For example, let us assume you started out as a meter reader for a large electric utility. One would at first assume that your productivity would be measured by the number of meters you could read correctly in a given time. This is basically true, but it doesn't stop there. There is the matter of how you get along with homeowners or customers and, even more important, how your supervisor and the other employees react to you.

In other words, a meter reader is never just a meter reader. He is a member of a team. He is a potential supervisor. He is a potential manager. He is also a potential drawback to the company if he doesn't handle things properly. And as far as his advancement is concerned, his human relations ability may be as important as his job performance, providing, of course, that he is above average in this respect.

Let us take the example of a checker in a supermarket. The productivity of a checker is usually measured in three ways: speed, accuracy, and relations with customers. But it doesn't stop there. Why? Because the way others react to him has an influence on *their* productivity as well as his own. If he is an excellent checker and measures above others in all three categories, one would think he would be the best checker of all. But would he be? Not necessarily.

Let us assume that it is a peak period in the supermarket and all checkers are extremely busy. Shoppers are lined up in front of each check stand. One of the checkers suddenly runs out of paper sacks and calls for our "superior" checker to toss him a few. What if our checker says, "Come and get 'em if you want 'em"? What would happen? A psychological barrier would immediately arise between the two checkers. The checker requesting the bags would be embarrassed in front of his customers, and, as a result, his speed, his accuracy, and his relations with his customers would deteriorate. So even though our superior checker is superior in all three categories, he has hurt the total productivity of the operation. Nobody can beat him as far as doing his *assigned* job is concerned; it is just that he is not "human relations smart."

A third example might be a teller in a bank. Suppose a young woman is fast, accurate, and effective with customers. In fact, she is so good that she attracts more customers to her window and as a result carries a very high work load in comparison with the other tellers. But she has a haughty attitude. She doesn't mix with the other girls. Consequently, the other tellers build up resentment toward her, and their productivity is lowered. In this example it is conceivable that the young teller actually hurts the efficiency of the department *even though her personal productivity is the highest.*

In other words, productivity is not only what you do yourself; it is also the influence, good or bad, you have on others. The worker who keeps his personal productivity high and at the same time is sensitive enough to have a beneficial influence on others is the one management will eventually reward. You not only have a job to perform; you have a contribution to make to your fellow employees. It is not a contribution that always comes easy. On occasion you may find it necessary to work effectively with someone you do not like. If you succeed, you have accepted a difficult challenge and you have made a worthwhile contribution. If you fail, at least try to learn something from the experience and wait for another chance, for it is a contribution that you *must* eventually make.

Human relations knows no age or experience level. Whether you are a recent high school or college graduate entering the employ of a large electric company, a widow of fifty entering the labor market for the first time, a senior citizen taking up the selling of mutual funds, a housewife returning to a secretarial job she left ten years ago, or a long-time career employee only five years from retirement, human relations will play a vital role in the years that lie ahead.

Once you understand that there is no escape from human relations, you will be in a position to accept the challenge and earn the right to receive the greatest compliment of all. This will, we hope, happen sometime in your immediate future when a supervisor or a fellow employee refers to you as being "human relations smart."

8

PROBLEM

1

Rod Faces Reality

Rod was very pleased with himself when he, along with two other equally qualified fellows, landed a job with the Southern Electrical Company. It was a strong organization with an excellent reputation. He started his new job with high spirits and a promise to himself that he would do his very best.

After successfully completing his three months probationary period, Rod was assigned to a department that was known for its high productivity and outstanding teamwork. Before the first day was over Rod's supervisor told him how lucky he was to win the assignment and then quietly suggested to him that he make a special effort to be friendly and get along with everybody.

Rod worked hard and efficiently in his new assignment, but he made a series of obvious human relations mistakes. He was a little impatient with one co-worker who was late in returning some equipment. He complained one morning when his coffee break was delayed because he had to wait for another fellow to return from his. He was openly upset one day when his work load was temporarily increased because a fellow employee had to go home sick.

After a few weeks had passed, the supervisor called Rod into his office and had a second, more serious talk with him. He pointed out that everybody needed to work very closely together in a department of this kind and that Rod would contribute more if he made more of an effort to become one of the team. At the end of the interview, Rod asked if his work was satisfactory. The supervisor told him it was substantially above average.

Some months later Rod heard that the two men who were employed at the same time he was had received promotions.

He passed it off by saying, "In this outfit it isn't what you know but who you know that counts."

Was Rod justified in feeling this way? (For suggested answer, see page 198.)

2

"Don't ask me . . . I just work here."

Human Relations Can Make or Break You

Now that you have read the first chapter, perhaps you have a few questions you would like to ask. With your permission we will create a third party to ask your questions for you.

Meet Joe Harvey.

Joe has just finished college and is scheduled to report to work with a large industrial company the first of the month. He has made up his mind to carve out a real career for himself with this organization. He was married during his junior year and his wife is expecting their second child. You can see that Joe has reason to be serious about his first real career opportunity.

O.K., Joe, you are in the driver's seat. Fire away with your questions.

I am a rather quiet and timid person. Does this mean that I must work harder than others to be good at human relations?

It may. Many people who are supersensitive about being friendly and communicating with others need to make a special effort at the beginning to get over their unfounded fears. You cannot build good relationships with people if you withdraw into your shell and refuse to give them a chance to know you. People who are very quiet and self-sufficient sometimes forget that their silence may be interpreted as aloofness, indifference, or even hostility. To avoid this possibility you must learn to communicate frequently and openly with the people you work with. It should be encouraging for you to know, however, that many young people who start out in a timid manner become highly skilled at human relations later on, because the very sensitivity that caused them to be timid in the beginning helps them to be more aware of the needs of others.

This is a tough question, but how can I build greater inner confidence in approaching people so that I can start building good working relationships with them?

You must gamble and take the first step instead of standing on the sidelines and thinking about it. This means that you must greet your fellow workers pleasantly even though you occasionally might be ignored; it means you must talk with people even though you feel clumsy about it and feel that what you say might be rejected. Of course, taking such initiative may occasionally cause a brief moment of embarrassment, but with experience you will sense a new inner confidence that will make it much easier for you in the future.

Will paying more attention to human relations give me a brighter future?

Your question deserves an unqualified yes answer, Joe. Most management experts agree that those employees who concentrate on good human relations get the best jobs and slowly rise to the top in most organizations. Those who do not pay much attention to human relations seem to get lost and are pushed into the least desirable jobs. All organizations are built around people, and when you build healthy relationships with your fellow workers and supervisors, you open doors that would otherwise be closed. Look at it this way, Joe. You have a good education; you have a high potential; you have the desire to succeed. All of this is great, but you can't put it to work unless you work well with people, because, if they want to, they can put up road blocks at every corner. Whether you accept it or not, people will control your job future, and the better the relationships you build with them the better things will be for you.

How much human relations skill must I have to move ahead quickly?

The more the better, of course, but not as much as you might suspect. It is surprising how many capable people ignore the importance of human relations, making it easier for those who don't. Only a few people actually take time to think seriously about human relations. You are different. By reading this book you are concentrating on the problem. You are taking time to study the subject and become more knowledgeable about it. This effort on your part should help you be more satisfied with your job and move ahead more quickly.

Why is human relations more important to the worker today than it was thirty or forty years ago?

There are many reasons, Joe, Here are five of the most important ones:

1. Business, industrial, and governmental organizations are larger, more complex, and consequently more dependent on *group* effort than they were years ago. In the old days, more employees worked in isolated jobs than they do today. More interpersonal relationships are necessary in a modern business enterprise.

2. Today more workers are employed in service occupa-

tions. Customer relations are an important part of most business organizations, because the future of the organization depends on how well the customer is served. This makes human relations more important throughout the company.

3. There are fewer unskilled jobs in our society today. Years ago people were hired to do routine work that is done today by machines. They did the isolated specific task and had little to say. There are very few of those jobs left. Most have been replaced by jobs involving close association with other workers.

4. Management has discovered that greater productivity is the key to greater profit and an increase in the standard of living for all people. This is the keystone of the modern free-enterprise system. In order to gain greater productivity, people must get along better.

5. Although there is still a long way to go, more and more supervisors are being trained in the elements of good human relations. Because of this many are more sensitive to the behavior of those working for them. This causes the supervisor to expect more from the worker in the human relations sense.

Is human relations as important in small organizations as it is in large ones?

Generally speaking, yes. The size of an organization is not important insofar as getting along with people is concerned. There are some important differences, though. Your progress, over a long period, may depend more on good human relations in a large company than in a small company. This is true because there is more supervision and more human relations responsibility in a large company. Some higher positions are almost exclusively leadership positions, where human relations is 60 or 70 percent of the total job. Remember that most people—some estimate as high as 70 percent—seek careers with large companies. Of course there are still excellent opportunities with organizations of a hundred employees or less. At the same time, large companies are getting larger. Mergers are more common than ever before.

The big companies were the first to introduce human relations training for supervisors. They are likely to place more importance on it. It follows that because smaller companies may not provide as much training and assistance, you may have to be more human relations smart on your own.

Will becoming human relations smart help me become a supervisor sooner?

Emphatically, yes.

The way you play your human relations cards will strongly influence your progress toward a position of supervisory responsibility, should this be your goal. There are of course other factors, such as your mental ability and your willingness to work, which will also play an important role. But the daily application of the tips and techniques you receive in this book will unquestionably help you. Put another way, few employees who do not become human relations smart reach a position of leadership.

What is meant by the term "human relations smart"? Does this mean I must have high mental ability to become smart in this sense?

No! You may have high mental ability (measured in terms of IQ) and still not be human relations smart. There appears to be little or no correlation between high mental ability and the ability to work well with people. In fact, some individuals with very high mental ability appear to be human relations dumb. People and the way they react are not always important to these individuals. They often do not want to be bothered. They sometimes make wonderful research people, but usually they are poor supervisors.

Does a person have to be an extrovert to be human relations smart?

No. An extrovert is a person who is outgoing and likes to be around people. He is usually an individual who speaks up freely. We find that many people who are very quiet and calm are still very smart in dealing with others.

Human relations is *sensitivity* to others, and extroverts are often too concerned with themselves to be good in building relations with others. The skills and principles outlined in this book can be learned and applied by both extroverts and introverts.

Why are some people so obviously awkward or dumb at human relations?

That's a tough question, Joe, because each personality is different and there could be many complex reasons. Here are a few possibilities. Some individuals are so self-centered that they think only of themselves and therefore give little consideration to the feelings of others; some are blinded by ambition to the point that they gamble with their relationships with others and frequently lose; and some let their emotions temporarily spill over, thus destroying relationships they have carefully built in the past. Of course, there are those who are simply insensitive to the people around them, and, unless they receive special counseling or training that develops awareness, they never come to understand why they have more human problems than other people. It may be hard to admit, but we all make more human relations mistakes than we should. We are all human relations dumb now and then. You'll never be perfect at handling these problems, but you should never stop trying to improve your abilities to deal effectively with others.

Is high performance in school a guarantee of high performance on the job?

No. An individual can be outstanding in an academic way but be very weak in actual performance on the job, because the work environment is different, people are different, and the objectives in business are different from those in the classroom. It is frequently true that a student who is average in the classroom is outstanding on the job, and vice versa. This can mean that some students who are high achievers academically might have more of an adjustment to make to the world of work than those who get more practical experience along the way.

Will I have to change my personality to become human relations smart?

Your basic personality need not be changed. However, you can change many of your habits, attitudes, and approaches in working with people. You can, to a limited extent, change your behavior. It would be foolish to say you can or should change your basic personality. You are what you are, and you cannot be someone else. If you develop the personality you already have by using better human relations, your progress will be rewarding beyond all your expectations. In other words, all the suggestions in this book can be used within the framework of your own personality.

Will this book really help me become human relations smart?

If you give it a chance, yes. But first you must accept the ideas presented here as sound and in keeping with your sense of dignity. Your biggest job, of course, will be to apply what you learn on your present job. If you put an idea or technique into practice long enough, it becomes a habit and you do it automatically. It won't be easy, and naturally no book of this kind can have all the answers. No one is ever human relations perfect. Your problem is not to become perfect but to become substantially better than your competitors. This will make the *difference* you need to become successful.

Human behavior does not change easily. Modification of attitudes and habits is a slow, difficult process. Whether you make these changes will depend on how badly you wish to succeed. This book tells you *how* to become human relations smart.

The rest is up to you.

PROBLEM

2

The Case of Miss Katy

Katy and Ann were both young and very attractive. They joined the M.K. Company on the same day and went through the same training program in preparation for identical jobs involving a great deal of close contact with fellow employees.

Although it was not easy, Ann made a good adjustment to her work environment. She was able to do this because of her warm, flexible personality and her willingness to accept people enthusiastically. In a few cases she took the initiative in building relationships with a few older employees. Within a few weeks she was relaxed and happy. There were no strangers left.

Katy, on the other hand, made little progress in adjusting to her new work environment. She appeared rigid and distant to those who worked around her. To a few she even seemed aloof and hostile. Katy's supervisor, watching her from a distance, felt Katy was waiting around expecting others to approach her and be friendly. She seemed to be standing on the sidelines, unable or unwilling to meet people half way.

A few weeks later, during lunch, Katy told Ann she was going to look for another job. Her reasons were as follows: (1) She felt everyone was unfriendly. (2) She resented some of her fellow employees, especially a few older women, who seemed to be extremely critical of her. (3) She felt her supervisor was trying to push her into a mold of conformity that was simply not her style. Why should she go all out to be friendly? After all, building working relationships is a two-way thing. She felt confident that she could find another company that would appreciate her more and give her all the freedom she needed to be herself.

What chance do you feel Katy had of finding a job environment that would make her completely happy? (For suggested answer, see page 199.)

CHAPTER

3

"I'll keep my positive attitude."

Hold on to Your Positive Attitude

Attitude is a very common word. You hear it almost every day. Parents talk about it at home. Teachers use it in classes. Supervisors discuss it at work. Sometimes it seems overused. Yet no other word will have more impact on your future. This is true because your positive attitude is your most priceless personal possession.

If you can create and keep a positive attitude toward your job, your company, and life in general, you will not only move up the ladder of success quickly and gracefully, but you will also be a happier person. If you are unable to do this, you will find many doors closed to you on the job, and your personal and social life will be something less than exciting.

Who evaluates your
is it always valid
other – adapting to accepted attitude –
Maverick

Because attitude will play such an important role in your
future, let's take a close look at the meaning and connotation
of the word itself.

Attitude is defined by most psychologists as a mental set
that will cause you to respond in a characteristic manner
to a given stimulus. A more sophisticated definition is given
by G. W. Allport, a prominent social psychologist:

> An attitude is a mental and neural state of readiness,
> organized through experience, exerting a directive and dy-
> namic influence upon the individual's response to all ob-
> jects and situations with which it is related.

modify

You have, in effect, many attitudes or mental sets in your
mind. You have your favorite colors. If red is your favorite
color, you have a favorable attitude toward things that are
red; if green is not attractive to you, we might say you have
a mental set against things that are green.

We could carry this idea of mental sets on and on. You
have attitudes toward certain makes of automobiles, toward
certain social institutions (schools, churches, and the like),
toward careers, toward life styles, and toward people.

The important thing as far as this book is concerned is
that you will develop attitudes on your new job. You will
build attitudes toward your supervisor and the people you
work with, toward the job you do, toward company policies,
and, among other things, toward the amount of money you
are being paid. In addition to these specific attitudes, you
will also have a basic, or total, attitude toward your job and,
in a larger sense, toward life itself. It might be more accurate
to call this a philosophy, but because the word attitude is
used so often to mean a total outlook, we must understand
it in this sense also. Strictly speaking, when we use the term
attitude in this larger sense, we can say that attitude is *the
way you look at your environment.*

Strangely enough, it seems (at least to some extent) that
you can look at the world around you in any way you wish.
If you wish to see all the seamy, unpleasant things in life,
you can focus your attention on them. If, on the other hand,
you prefer to see the more beautiful and inspirational things
in life, you can focus your attention on them.

training
environment
experience

Attitude is a matter of perception. There are of course many pleasant things in life, and many unpleasant things. Some people seem to have the capacity to push the unpleasant things out of their perception—or to the outer perimeter of their thinking—and dwell most of the time on the pleasant things. Others seem to enjoy the unpleasant and dwell on these factors.

What you see in life influences your attitude.

If you go around looking for what is wrong with things, wondering why things are not better, and complaining about them, then you will be a negative person in the minds of most people. If you do the opposite—look for what is good and don't focus on unpleasant things—you will be a positive person in the minds of most people.

Every job has certain unfavorable or negative things about it. There is no perfect job or position. One job may have more favorable things about it than another, but all jobs have *some* unpleasant things. The employee who dwells on the unfavorable factors has a negative attitude. If he forces himself to look for factors that are favorable, he will slowly become a more positive person.

If you start your new job with a positive attitude, our concern then is whether it will remain positive. It is possible that you will meet a few people on your work assignment who have negative attitudes and will attempt to persuade you to think as they do. You no doubt will find a few factors about the job itself that are negative.

To be a positive person, you need not think your company is perfect. This would be foolish. You would eventually become disillusioned. On the other hand, unless you feel that the majority of factors are favorable, you will eventually become negative, and you will show it.

There is another way to look at it. Once you focus your attention more on the negative factors than on the positive, you are hurting yourself and your chances in the future.

The moment you can no longer be positive about your career with your company, your chances for success diminish.

No one, of course, can be positive all the time. You will have periods of doubt. These temporary periods of evaluation will not seriously hurt you. But a day-to-day negative attitude that persists over weeks and months will destroy your future with the company. If this should happen, and you honestly feel such an attitude is justified, you should resign.

A positive attitude is essential to career success for many reasons.

1. When you are positive you are usually more energetic, highly motivated, productive, and alert. Apparently, thinking about negative things too much has a way of draining your energy. Put another way, a positive attitude seems to open a gate that lets your inner enthusiasm spill out; a negative attitude, on the other hand, seems to keep the gate closed.

2. First impressions are important on the job because they often have a lasting quality. People you meet for the first time appear to have little radar sets tuned in to your attitude. If your attitude is positive, they receive a friendly, warm signal, and they are attracted to you; if your attitude is negative, they receive an unfriendly signal, and they try to avoid you.

3. A positive employee contributes to the productivity of others; a negative employee does not. Attitudes are caught more than they are taught! Both negative and positive attitudes are transmitted on the job; they are caught or picked up by others. A persistently negative attitude, like the rotten apple in the barrel, can spoil the positive attitudes of others. It is very difficult to maintain a high level of productivity while working next to a person with a negative attitude.

4. People like you when you are positive. They like to be around you, because you are fun. This makes your job more interesting and exciting, because you are in the middle of things and not on the outside complaining. When you are negative, people prefer to stay clear of you. A negative person may build good relationships with a few other people (who are perhaps negative themselves), but he cannot build good relationships with the majority of employees.

5. The kind of attitude you transmit to management will have a great deal to do with your future success. Management constantly reads your mental attitude, even though you may feel you are successful in covering it up. Supervisors can determine your attitude by your approach to your job, your reaction to directives, the way you handle problems, and especially

by the way you work with others, including customers. If you are positive you will be given greater consideration when special assignments and promotional opportunities arise.

As you take a closer look at your own positive attitude, it is important that you realize that a positive attitude is far more than a smile.

Not that there is anything wrong with a smile. Far from it! But a smile is only one manifestation of an inner positive attitude. In fact, some people transmit a positive attitude even though they seldom smile. They do this by the way they treat others, the way they look at their responsibilities, and the perspective they take when faced with a problem.

Attitude is a highly personal thing. It is very close to your ego, to the way you look at yourself. Because of this, attitude is a very touchy subject. It is not easy to talk about. People freeze when the word is mentioned. As a result, management may never talk to you about your attitude. They may never say to an employee, "Joe, let's be honest. Your attitude is negative. What are you going to do about it?"

Don't expect someone to send you a message when your attitude is showing. You wouldn't like it. You wouldn't accept it. As a matter of fact, you probably wouldn't permit anyone to really talk to you about your attitude.

But everyone will know when it is showing.

How, then, do you make sure you keep your positive attitude when things get tough? How do you keep a good grip on it when you are discouraged? How do you keep it in good repair on a day-to-day basis over the years?

Here are a few simple suggestions.

1. Remember that your positive or negative attitude is not something that you can hang on a hook and forget when you report to work or return home. It follows you wherever you go. It is reasonable to assume then that if you make a greater effort to be a more positive person in your social and personal life, this will automatically spill over and help you on the job. By the same token, if you make a greater effort to develop a more positive attitude at work, this will in turn make a contribution to your social and personal life. One effort will complement the other. People are people, so

if you can build a more positive attitude in one environment, you will become more successful in another.

2. Negative comments are seldom welcomed by fellow workers on the job; neither are they welcomed by those you meet in the social scene. The solution? Talk about positive things. Be complimentary. Constant gripers and complainers do not build healthy and exciting relationships with anybody.

3. Look for the good things in the people you work with, especially your supervisors. Nobody is perfect, but almost everybody has a few worthwhile qualities. If you dwell on people's good features it will be easier for you to like them and easier for them to like you. Make no mistake about one thing: *people know how you react to them whether you communicate your attitude verbally or not.*

4. Look for the good things in your department. What are the factors that make it a good place to work? Do you like the hours, the physical environment, the people, the actual work you are doing, the atmosphere? Of course, you are not expected to like everything. No department or work assignment is perfect. But, if you concentrate on the good things, the negative factors will seem less important and will not bother you as much. This does not mean that you should ignore negative elements that should be changed. Far from it! A positive person is not a weak person. You are not expected to submit to all factors in your work environment. Management is not seeking passive people who meekly conform. They want spirited, positive people who will make improvements.

5. Look for the good things in your company. Just as there are no perfect departments, there are no perfect companies. Nevertheless, almost all organizations have many good features. Is your company progressive? What about promotional opportunites? Do you have chances for self-improvement? What about your wage and benefit package? Do you have the freedom you seek? You cannot expect to have everything you would like, but there should be enough to keep you positive. If there isn't, you should look elsewhere. If you decide to stick with a company for a long period of time, you would be smart to look at the good features and think about them. If you think positively, you will act positively, and soon you will be sufficiently successful to be glad you stuck it out.

6. Don't permit a fellow worker (or even a supervisor) who has a negative attitude to trap you into his way of thinking. You may not be able to change his attitude, but at least you can protect your own positive attitude from becoming negative. The story of Sandy will emphasize this point.

Sandy was a little uneasy about starting her new job. It was a fine opportunity and she knew the standards were very high. Would she have the skills needed? Could she learn fast enough to please her supervisor? Would the older employees like her? Although Sandy's concern was understandable, it was not justified. In addition to being highly qualified for the job, she also had a happy, positive attitude that wouldn't stop. She was seldom depressed.

Everything went very well for Sandy for awhile. Her positive attitude was appreciated by all. Slowly, however, her fellow workers and supervisor noticed a change. She became more critical of her colleagues, her job, and the company. Her usual friendly greetings and helpful ideas were gradually replaced by complaints. What had happened? Without realizing it, Sandy was showing the effects of friendships she had made. Needing acceptance in a strange environment, she had welcomed the attention of a clique of girls who had a negative attitude—a group that management already viewed critically.

Sandy was not able to confine her negative attitude to her job. Soon, again without realizing it, she let her negative attitude spill over into her social life. In fact, it troubled her boyfriend so much that he had it out with her one night. His words were a little rough. "Look, Sandy. When you are happy you are very attractive and fun to be around. But frankly, when you are negative, you are a real bore and I never have a good time with you. I think those girls you hang around with on the job are killing what was once a beautiful personality." It wasn't a happy evening, but Sandy got the message. She pulled away slowly from her negative friends, salvaged her positive attitude, and saved her future with the company.

The following little saying may help you hold on to your positive attitude. You may wish to copy it down on a small card and use it as a reminder. If you read it over and over, it will make you very aware of what we have talked about in this chapter.

YOUR ATTITUDE SPEAKS SO LOUDLY I CAN'T HEAR WHAT YOU HAVE TO SAY.

There are three forms of communication between people. One is the written form—a note, a letter, a memo, or a telegram. Then there is the verbal form—face-to-face conversation, telephone conversation, or intercom discussion.

These forms of communication are so important to the operation of an organization that we tend to think they are the only ones. We often forget the third form—the transmission of our attitudes. We forget that something psychologically very important takes place between people even without the written or spoken word. We also communicate through facial expressions, hand gestures, and other more subtle forms of body language. So every time you report for work, every time you attend a staff meeting, every time you take a coffee break, and every time you go out socially, make life better for yourself by remembering that . . .

Your attitude is showing!

PROBLEM

3

Manuel's Changing Attitude

Manuel was an art major in high school and through two years of college. He was a highly sensitive individual with considerable talent. His art teachers constantly praised his work, and he won a number of prizes in campus showings.

Upon graduating from his community college, he made many attempts to find a job in commercial art. No luck. After many disappointments, he reluctantly accepted a position with a large retail chain that would only have limited use for his talent in the area of merchandising display.

Manuel decided to make the most of his situation and began his career with a positive attitude. He quickly demonstrated that he had both talent and managerial ability. His future looked bright. He was happy.

Some time later, however, Manuel's supervisor noticed a definite change in his attitude. Manuel's enthusiasm started to dwindle. He began giving excuses for not getting things done. His displays were not up to standard. His relationships with people began to deteriorate.

The manager had two heart-to-heart talks with Manuel, but a change in attitude and productivity was not forthcoming. This continued for over a year. One day, in desperation, the manager gave Manuel his two-week notice. That night, over a few beers, Manuel said to one of his close friends: "I should have resigned a year ago on the very day I noticed my attitude changing. I've wasted a complete year."

Is it possible for a person to know the exact day or week his attitude changes? Did Manuel help or hurt himself by staying on the job even though his attitude and productivity deteriorated? Do you feel he was honest with himself or his manager? (For suggested answer, see page 200.)

"Relationships are that important?"

Vertical and Horizontal Working Relationships

When you meet a supervisor or fellow worker for the first time, a psychological reaction takes place: each person instantaneously interprets the other. It is a feeling you can't define. You know something is happening, but you can't put your finger on it. Slowly, as you and the other individual see each other more frequently and get to know each other better, these initial feelings mature into what is called a *relationship*.

A relationship is a *feeling thing* that exists between two people who associate with each other. You can't see, hear, taste, smell, or touch a relationship—you can only feel it in a psychological sense. Relationships that exist on the job are usually different from those you build in the social scene.

They are relationships that exist only because you selected a certain company and were assigned to work with certain people in a specific department. In other words, in your social life you have a choice; on the job you do not. Nevertheless, working relationships are extremely important to you and your future because they will have a strong influence on your personality and personal productivity, as well as on that of others.

Working relationships of this nature are fascinating to study. For example, one interesting characteristic is that two persons cannot meet regularly on the job or work in the same general areas *without* having a relationship. So the first thing to learn about working relationships is that whether you like it or not, one will exist between you and every employee or supervisor with whom you have regular contact.

You need not work geographically near this person.

You need not speak to him.

You need not even have a desire to know him.

Yet, a relationship will exist between you. The very fact that you might decide to ignore a person does not destroy the relationship; in fact, the opposite happens. The relationship becomes more tense and psychologically powerful. Let us take a specific example.

You notice an employee working in a department next to you. In an attempt to be friendly, you say hello in a very pleasant way to this person the first day on the job, and you receive no reply.

Does this mean the relationship is cut off at this point?

Far from it! You may feel that his failure to reply is a slight to you and be a little disturbed about it. You may decide not to take the initiative again. Nevertheless, you will remember this person clearly and wonder what will happen in the future.

The person to whom you said hello, on the other hand, has had some kind of reaction to your friendly gesture. He may feel that he treated you in an unfriendly manner (perhaps he was not feeling well on that day), and might welcome another opportunity to be more friendly. Or, he may have interpreted your hello as being a little too forward on your part as a new employee and decided to be cool toward you.

You could ignore him. You could avoid verbal contact. You and he could see each other only a few times each week.

Would a relationship exist?

Yes, indeed. Two persons have made contact with each other. They see each other occasionally. They work for the same company. As long as these factors exist, a relationship must exist. Under these conditions you cannot erase a relationship. The attempt on the part of one person to withdraw serves only to make the relationship more emotionally charged; it does not in any manner eliminate it.

You cannot work with or near people or communicate with them without having relationships with them.

There is another interesting characteristic about these relationships when viewed objectively. They are either strong or weak, warm or cool, healthy or unhealthy, friendly or distant. There is no middle-of-the-road or neutral ground. Every relationship has either some positive content or some negative content.

Have you ever heard someone say "I can take her or leave her"? The phrase usually means that it doesn't make any difference whether the person referred to is around or not. But the very fact that one makes such a comment indicates that it would be better if the person were not around. The relationship still exists, and in this case it is a little cool.

A third characteristic is that each relationship is different. You must build relationships with all kinds of people, regardless of race, religion, age, sex, and personality characteristics. Each relationship will be unique. Each will be built on a different basis. Each will have its own integrity.

As you look around and study your co-workers and your supervisor, it is easy to see that they are all different. They are all separate personalities. Even so, some individuals believe that *they* look the same to everyone around them. In other words, from the other side of the relationship, do you look the same to others?

Strange as it may seem, you do not.

You do not look the same to different people. Just as other people appear different to you, you appear different to other people. You make a different impression on each of them because they interpret you differently.

There is another way of saying this: You do not have a *single* personality in the eyes of others. Because each person interprets you differently (based on his own unique background, prejudices, likes, dislikes, and so on), your personality, to that person, is different. The way he interprets your personality *is* your personality to that person.

If you were to stand up for ten minutes in front of ten total strangers, and if each of them were invited to write out in detail how he interpreted your personality, what kind of personality sketches would you receive? Would they be the same? Would they be different? To be sure, they might all be favorable sketches, but they would not be the same. Each person would describe you as a slightly different person.

When you stop to think about it, the way things are now in your on-the-job situation is very similar to the way things were when you were a student on campus. Even then you were frequently misinterpreted by your teachers, parents, and friends; you had problems with people of all varieties, even with a few of your very close friends. No matter what you did to try and change it, people continued to see you—and your personality—in their own peculiar way.

Why all this emphasis on the way in which people view your personality? How will this help the ambitious person in his efforts to be human relations smart?

Here is your answer: Because everybody sees you differently, you will have to build good relationships with different people differently. And make no mistake here. *Good relationships must be built.* They seldom come about automatically.

You will rarely build a strong, warm, or healthy relationship with two persons in the same way. You will always have to take into consideration the party at the other end of the relationship. Each person you build a working relationship with should be studied and evaluated on an individual basis.

Some people are not going to interpret your personality favorably to start with. You are going to have to be smart enough to determine who these people are, and then you must build a good relationship with them on an individual basis. It is not easy to change a cool relationship to a warm one, yet you cannot afford to allow it to remain in an unhealthy state. You must make some effort to convert it to a stronger relationship. To do this, you must first study the person at the other end of the relationship, and remember that he sees you differently than anyone else in the world does. With this in mind, you can plan a strategy that may produce good results. Other chapters in this book will give you specific help in this respect.

Now that you have a good picture of just what is meant by a relationship, it is time to talk about the two kinds of relationships.

First we will discuss the *vertical working relationship.*

This is the relationship between you and your immediate supervisor. If you have two or more supervisors, you will have two or more vertical relationships to create and maintain. Normally, you will have one immediate supervisor, as illustrated below.

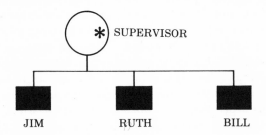

In a small department consisting of one supervisor and three employees, each employee has a different vertical relationship with the same supervisor. This relationship is indicated by the line between each employee and the supervisor. This is often called the *job-relations line.* If the relationship is strong, we indicate this by a heavy line. If it is weak, we indicate this by a light line. Naturally, it is almost impossible for the supervisor to create and maintain an equally strong line between himself and all employees in the department. It is his job to try to do this, and the closer he comes to this ideal the better it is for the department. But supervisors are human beings and are not perfect; consequently, the job-relations lines are seldom equally strong. The person working next to you might have a stronger relationship with the supervisor than you have, or he might have a weaker one.

You will notice in the illustration below that arrows have been added to the lines.

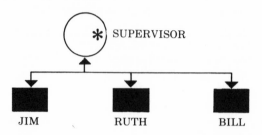

These arrows at the ends of the vertical job-relations lines have real significance. They signify that there should be a free flow of information between the workers and the supervisor. A strong relationship cannot exist between two persons without two-way communication. The supervisor must feel free to discuss, openly and frankly, certain problems with Jim, Ruth, and Bill. If the supervisor hesitates to talk with Jim about a certain weakness in his job performance, the relationship between the two of them is not what it could be. By the same token, if Jim is hesitant about taking a suggestion or a gripe to the supervisor, the relationship is less than ideal.

The lifeblood of a good relationship is free and open communication.

Good relationships are built and maintained by free and frequent verbal communication. People must talk with each other, exchange ideas, voice complaints, and offer suggestions if they intend to keep a good relationship. The moment that one party refuses to talk things over, the relationship line becomes thin and weak.

The primary responsibility for creating and maintaining a strong vertical relationship rests with the supervisor. This is a responsibility that goes with his position. If the relationship line is in need of repair, it is primarily his responsibility to initiate a discussion that can mend the break.

Although the supervisor has the primary responsibility, you as the employee have the secondary responsibility to keep the relationship line strong and healthy. Some employees make the serious mistake of thinking that the supervisor has one hundred percent of the responsibility to make the employee happy and productive.

A later chapter will be devoted to showing you how to create and maintain a good relationship with your supervisor; it will suffice now to say that you can't expect the supervisor to do all the relationship building. You will have to work hard to keep a good job-relations line between yourself and the supervisor. Even if you have an exceptionally poor supervisor, you'll have to meet him halfway. Vertical relationships must be in healthy repair if productivity is to be high in a department. Often the supervisor finds it a very delicate matter to keep it that way. Small wonder that management has seen fit to give him some special training.

The *horizontal working relationship* is as important to you as the vertical relationship. In fact, it is often more important. Horizontal working relationships are those that exist between you and fellow workers in the same department—the people you work next to on an hour-to-hour, day-to-day basis. The diagram below illustrates the horizontal relationships between three people in a very small department.

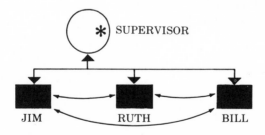

You will note that Jim has a horizontal working relationship with both Ruth and Bill. In this very small department of three employees and one supervisor, Jim has one vertical relationship and two horizontal relationships to keep strong. It is easy to see that in larger departments there would be many more. In fact, the larger the department you are assigned to, the more horizontal working relationships you must build and maintain.

You (not the supervisor) have the primary responsibility for creating and keeping healthy horizontal relationships. The supervisor—working at a long distance in regard to these relationships—has the secondary responsibility. He might find it necessary to step in once in a while to help restore a good relationship between two employees, but, by and large, he must leave these up to the employees themselves. He is more an arbitrator when it comes to horizontal relationships.

The critical need for building good horizontal working relationships is often ignored by some workers. When they permit this to happen, their doors of opportunity are locked and the keys are thrown away. *Nothing is more important to the new employee than building and maintaining good horizontal working relationships.* In fact, this should be a major part of your total human relations effort as you start your career. Much of this book is devoted to the principles and techniques that will assist you in this respect. For example, here are two fatal mistakes you should avoid at any cost.

1. Avoid concentrating on building a good relationship with your supervisor at the expense of good horizontal relationships with your fellow workers.

2. Avoid concentrating on building one or two very strong horizontal working relationships at the expense of good relationships with the remaining fellow workers in your department.

Making either mistake will cause immediate disharmony in your department and will put you in human relations hot water. The supervisor cannot afford to have an extremely strong relationship with you and weak relationships with your fellow workers if he wants high productivity from all. It makes for dissension and immediate cries of favoritism. From your point of view, then, an overstrong vertical relationship can cause a general weakening of your horizontal working relationships. When you make the mistake of concentrating on one or two horizontal working relationships, the remaining horizontal relationships deteriorate and your vertical relationship with the supervisor is also weakened. *All working relationships should be given equal attention and consideration.* One should not be strengthened at the expense of others, even though it may be more fun and more satisfying. Balance is important.

There is an excellent principle of good human relations that you might follow in this regard: *When you concentrate on creating good horizontal working relationships with all fellow workers, you almost always automatically create a good vertical relationship with your supervisor.*

It should be recognized, of course, that the success of this principle is assured only if the supervisor is sufficiently sensitive to know what is going on. In the majority of cases this is a fair assumption. A perceptive supervisor will greatly appreciate any employee who builds a better team spirit in his department by creating and maintaining strong horizontal working relationships.

There are of course important relationships other than those indicated in the diagram. Your relationship-building activity should not be confined to a single department. For example, your supervisor has a boss and you should also build a good relationship with him. In addition, you should also develop relationships with other employees in other departments. You can even create good relationships with managers and supervisors in departments that are only indirectly connected with your own. You should pay special attention to creating friendly relationships with those people in the personnel department. You should also be careful not to neglect relationships with caretakers, custodians, guards, switchboard operators, secretaries, and many other people with whom you will have only limited contact. It is a good idea for you to expand your sphere of influence as quickly as possible on your new job. The more good relationships you build, the better.

As important as these peripheral relationships may be, however, they are not your primary working relationships. You must build such relationships on an occasional or supplementary basis. Chance contacts, interdepartmental staff meetings, and telephone conversations are some of the opportunities that will give you a chance to do this. You cannot, however, afford to concentrate on building relationships outside your department by neglecting those on the inside.

The building of a strong vertical relationship with your immediate supervisor and strong horizontal working relationships with your fellow workers is absolutely essential to your personal success. No other human relations activity should have a higher priority.

PROBLEM

4

The Aloof Supervisor

Bernie received his first assignment two days after joining the Elite Company. He was to be the junior member of the traffic department in which he would have seven horizontal relationships and one vertical relationship to build. All of the other employees, including the supervisor, were much older than he was.

After one week in the department, he discovered that his supervisor was almost impossible to approach or talk to, that he stayed aloof from the workers in the department, and that he seemed generally negative and critical. In fact, Bernie could feel a strong psychological barrier between the supervisor and the rest of the department. Once a week there was a short staff meeting, but most of the employees were silent and somewhat hostile. For Bernie it was a tense and unfortunate situation.

How could he build a strong and worthwhile vertical relationship with a man of this nature in an environment that was anything but friendly? After giving it some serious thought, he decided to concentrate exclusively on horizontal relationships. The supervisor seemed to be a lost cause, so why should he make any direct efforts to build a relationship the supervisor didn't seem to want anyway?

What result might such an effort have had? Was this a smart decision on Bernie's part? Would you have gone about it differently? Support your point of view. (For suggested answer, see page 201.)

What's Super's Hang up? at some time in past He went thru the same route as B. (seek vunable area)

CHAPTER

5

"Some people aren't worth building relationships with!"

Productivity and Good Human Relations

Productivity, as we have seen, is a big word in the world of work. It is a rather sophisticated word that management uses a great deal. It is a word that we need to understand better.

A manufacturing plant, in order to be competitive with other operations turning out a similar product, must *produce* at the lowest possible cost per single item or unit; a retail store, in order to pay overhead expenses and show a profit, must *produce* sales at a certain level; an airline must *produce* a reliable service that will attract enough customers to keep the seats filled. Even a governmental organization, like a fire department, must *produce* at a level that will satisfy taxpayers so they will be willing to continue to pay the bills without complaints. Every kind of organization must produce, and when production is not sufficient to make a profit or satisfy people, changes are made. These are economic and political facts.

Management, therefore, must be interested not only in the productivity of individuals, but also in that of divisions, departments, or branches. They must be interested in order to survive. This is our free-enterprise system in operation.

Productivity is a difficult word to fully understand.

It means different things to different people, depending on the kind of organization one works for. Stated simply, it means on-the-job performance. The work you do. What you accomplish in an hour, a day, or a year.

Productivity for a salesperson in a department store means selling a certain amount of merchandise on a given day, doing a certain amount of stock work and clean-up activities, treating customers the right way, building good displays, and many other little things. Productivity not only means doing certain things; it also means *how* they are done.

Productivity to a needleworker in a garment factory may mean sewing on 780 sleeves according to specifications in an eight-hour period. If the needleworker sews 780 sleeves, she is a good producer; if she sews 860, she is an outstanding producer; if she sews 640, she is a poor producer.

Productivity to a telephone operator may mean handling a certain number of calls satisfactorily over a certain period.

Productivity depends on the job you have to do and the organization you work for. Regardless of the kind of job you have been assigned, however, you must produce.

Productivity is a management word.

Management uses it primarily as a word to indicate the output or performance of people, departments, or machines. Because all organizations must be interested in profits, management is always interested in ways of increasing productivity. Because an increase in costs (wages, materials, transportation, etc.) can only be offset by an increase in price or productivity, the emphasis is to be expected.

Why has management gone out of its way during the past

twenty years to improve employee cafeterias, lounge rooms, recreational facilities, lighting facilities, and countless other things?

There is but one answer: better employee morale that will result in greater productivity.

Because productivity is so important, management has devised ways of measuring it.

Productivity is easily measured on an assembly line where the worker must perform a specific function, such as connecting a wire or screwing on a nut. This kind of job can be time-studied and a certain standard rate can be established. If the standard rate is 85 completions in 60 minutes, it means that the average worker can reach and sustain this number over a certain period of time.

Measurable jobs or tasks of this nature are found primarily in the manufacturing and fabricating industries. Other jobs, such as that of a secretary, are more difficult to measure, because such factors as how much initiative is demonstrated, how people are treated, and how the telephone is answered must be considered. Productivity, then, can be measured scientifically in some situations, but in countless others it is measured by management judgment. Regardless of the kind of job you now hold or the way in which your productivity is measured, understanding what is meant by productivity (from the management point of view) is important to your future.

There are two kinds of productivity: individual productivity and group productivity. Individual productivity is a personal thing; it is the contribution a person makes under certain working situations to getting the job done. Group productivity is what a group can accomplish. It can be, and often is, measured objectively—that is, reduced to figures and statistics.

Each worker has a *current* (day-to-day, week-to-week) level of productivity that remains generally consistent, although it may fluctuate from period to period. To illustrate this, let's use a diagram of a glass or beaker. Let us assume that a solid line drawn across the glass is the *current* level of productivity for a person we will call Sam. Like all employees, Sam also has a *potential* level of productivity that is greater than his current level. Seldom, if ever, does a person reach

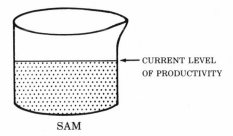

CURRENT LEVEL
OF PRODUCTIVITY

SAM

his full potential. Sam would be the first to agree that this is true. So let us draw a dotted line across the glass to indicate Sam's potential level of productivity. We don't know exactly where Sam's potential might be; it is impossible to measure his capacity or potential scientifically, because more than his mental ability is involved (and even his mental ability cannot be measured accurately). But for our hypothetical situation, we can say that his potential is substantially above his current level of productivity.

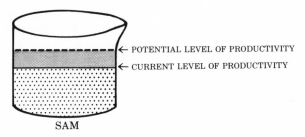

← POTENTIAL LEVEL OF PRODUCTIVITY
← CURRENT LEVEL OF PRODUCTIVITY

SAM

In the diagram below, then, Sam's current level of productivity is indicated by the solid line and his potential or possible level of productivity is indicated by the dotted line. The difference between the two is what we will call the *productivity gap*.

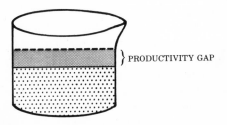

} PRODUCTIVITY GAP

There is always a gap between what one actually does and what one could do. Of course management would like to see Sam close the gap between his current and potential productivity levels as much as possible, but it would be asking too much to expect him to close it completely.

We are concerned, then, not so much with the gap itself as with the *size* of the gap. If it is small, Sam's supervisor knows he is working close to his capacity; if it is large, the supervisor knows that something is wrong and perhaps something should be done about it.

Sam's supervisor should, of course, do all he can to keep the distance between Sam's potential and his current performance as small as possible. If the gap becomes too great, he might decide Sam needs additional training, a special incentive, a change in assignment rotation, or perhaps some form of counseling. The supervisor cannot permit Sam's level of productivity to remain substandard over an extended period of time.

Sam, of course, is not the only worker in the department. In our imaginary situation, let us assume that there are two other employees occupying positions identical to Sam's. There would normally be many more than two, but in order to simplify our case we will include only Art and Fred.

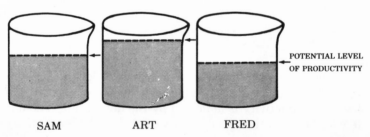

POTENTIAL LEVEL
OF PRODUCTIVITY

SAM   ART   FRED

You will note that the potentials of Art and Fred are different from Sam's. It is somewhat disturbing at first to recognize that everyone has his own potential and that some people have higher potentials than others. This is true because everyone has a different mental ability (IQ), ability to endure physical strain (stamina and endurance), ability to perform certain manipulative skills (aptitude), creative level, inner drive, and attitude, as well as other different personality characteristics. All of these features, added together, make up an individual's potential. Potential is much more than just mental ability.

It is important that you don't get hung up over the word *potential*. As we are using it, it simply means the level of productivity a worker might achieve under ideal circumstances if he were pushing himself to his limit. It is seldom, if ever, reached. In using the word *potential*, however, we should remember that some employees are outstanding in some areas, and average or below in others. Few, if any, have characteristics that make them outstanding in all areas. Yet almost everyone has at least one exceptional characteristic.

We need not be technical about the word. We need only to recognize that there are differences in capacity or potential between fellow workers. Some of it can be mental ability, but other characteristics also play an important role. Nor need we be concerned about the measurement of such levels for our purposes, because there is no scientific way to do this. All that we need be concerned about is that individual differences exist and that, except under extremely rare conditions, there is always a gap between one's potential and what one is presently achieving.

In the diagram to the left, Art has been arbitrarily given a potential above Sam's and Fred's. Fred, on the other hand, has been given a potential below Sam's and Art's.

Now, to complete our diagram, let us assign a current productivity level to each of the three workers.

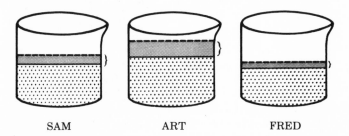

| SAM | ART | FRED |

You will note that even though Art has a higher potential than Sam, there is not a substantial difference between their current levels of performance. This is a compliment to Sam and perhaps indicates that he is more highly motivated to succeed and consequently performs closer to his potential.

Fred is also deserving of a compliment, because the gap between his current level of productivity and his potential is smaller than that for either Sam or Art. Fred is doing an excellent job in living up to his potential. Perhaps, with more education and training, Fred will be able to slowly raise his potential and, in turn, increase his productivity. In our hypothetical situation, however, Fred could not be expected to increase his productivity substantially.

If the reader studies this simple diagram, he will discover many provocative points of discussion. He can easily imagine the many variations and complications that would arise if the diagram were to include twelve employees instead of three. Even the premise that one can raise his potential through education and training is debatable. Our concern, however, is the relation between a person's occupational potential and his level of performance.

It is only natural that fellow employees should be compared with each other in respect to both potential and productivity.

It is only natural that they should compete among themselves.

It is only natural that management should be concerned with the gap between what an employee can do and what he is currently doing.

But individual productivity is not the only answer.

Just as each individual has a current and potential level of productivity, so does each branch, division, or department of an organization. This we call *group productivity.*

The diagram below illustrates this important concept. The

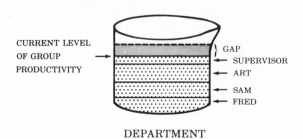

DEPARTMENT

glass or beaker represents the productivity level and potential of the department as a whole. Using Sam, Art, Fred, and the supervisor from our previous diagram, let us now combine their productivity in a departmental diagram.

You will observe that the productivity levels of Fred, Sam, and Art (from the previous chart) have been added together along with that of the supervisor. It is evident that the supervisor does not contribute as much in productivity (actually getting the work out) as do the individual employees. How could this be?

The answer is simple. The primary responsibility of the supervisor is to help each worker achieve *his* maximum productivity; the supervisor's secondary responsibility is (as a working supervisor) to get a certain amount of work done himself. He cannot be expected to take care of his many supervisory responsibilities and also do as much work as one of the employees in his department. His concern is *the total departmental productivity*, for this is how he is measured by management.

You will also notice that there is a gap in this chart just as there was in the others. This is a *departmental gap*. Just as an individual has a certain potential for productivity, so does a department. A crew of men working for a telephone company might have the potential of installing 120 telephones per day, and yet they might only install 80; a department inside a retail store might have the potential of selling $5,000 worth of merchandise on a given day when everything is ideal, and yet on most days they might sell only $2,000 worth; a claims department for an insurance company might have the potential to process 50 claims per day, and yet they may never reach this goal. Just as there is a gap with individuals, there is also one with departments.

It is the responsibility of the individual to try and close the gap between what he is currently producing and what he can ideally produce. It is the responsibility of the supervisor to close the gap between what his department is currently doing and what it might do in the future.

There are two ways in which he can do this. One is by working harder himself, putting in more hours and making better use of his time. Since he is only one person, there is a limit to what he could do by himself to reduce the size of the gap.

The second and by far the more effective way to reduce

the gap is to reduce the gaps between the levels of each of the three employees. The productivity of the department is the sum total of the productivity of all members of the department, including the supervisor. The supervisor is interested in each worker's productivity because of what each can contribute to the total.

What should this basic principle mean to you?

Simply this: All employees in a department are interdependent as far as departmental productivity is concerned. If you raise your personal productivity but at the same time, because of extremely poor human relations, take away some of the productivity of others in the department, you have not necessarily added to the total.

Sound strange?

To demonstrate this vital fundamental, let us take Art as an example. The diagram below tells us that Art has a high potential and a good level of personal productivity. In fact, he is currently producing a little more than Sam or Fred.

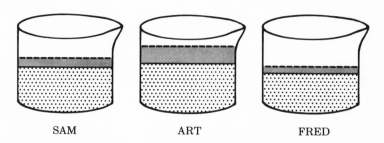

SAM   ART   FRED

But let us assume for a moment that Art begins to ignore Sam and Fred. He is no longer interested in helping them. He starts to rub them the wrong way. His superior attitude causes resentment.

What could happen then?

The productivity of Sam and Fred could drop due to departmental disharmony. The diagram at the top of the next page illustrates what might happen.

The gap between what Sam and Fred can do and what they are now doing has widened. Even though Art has maintained his *personal* level of productivity, *the departmental productivity level has dropped.*

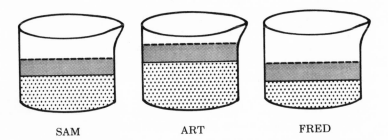

SAM   ART   FRED

Now let us see what might happen if Art does just the opposite. Let us assume that he becomes more human relations smart about his job. Instead of antagonizing Sam and Fred, he starts working with them on a better basis. He gives them some specific help on their off days; he compliments them on certain skills; he earns their respect instead of their animosity. Harmony replaces disharmony.

What could happen in this situation?

Again the diagram will give us a clear picture.

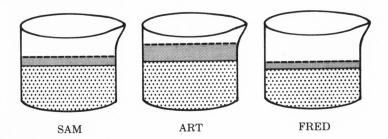

SAM   ART   FRED

Instead of a wider gap between the current and potential productivity levels of Sam and Fred, there is a smaller gap. Both Sam and Fred produce more because Art has strengthened his horizontal relationships with them. Instead of dropping, *the departmental productivity level has increased.*

This interdependence between workers in a department cannot be ignored. *Group* productivity is the key more than *individual* productivity.

Let's review what we have discussed in this chapter.

You have learned that there is always a gap between an individual's current level of productivity and his potential. If the employee consistently has a small gap, he is trying hard to contribute and should be complimented by his supervisor for working close to his potential.

You have learned that there is a departmental gap that represents the difference between what a department is doing and what it can do. If the departmental gap is small, the supervisor is doing a good job and should be complimented by his superiors.

You have also learned that because of the way people react to each other (human relations), one worker influences the productivity of others and therefore either lowers or increases the productivity of the entire department. In other words, it is possible for an employee to increase his *personal* productivity but decrease *departmental* productivity because of his poor human relations.

This may sound illogical or contradictory, but give it some serious thought. The sooner you start thinking the way management does, the sooner you will be ready to accept your human relations responsibility and start earning a management position for yourself.

PROBLEM

5

Jeff Misses the Message

Jeff was one of several employees in a small department where productivity depended upon the close cooperation of everyone involved. He had a high potential and lived up to it. Because of this, he personally produced more than anyone else in the department. But Jeff happened to be the kind of individual who liked to work alone. He was often aloof to others. He seldom volunteered to help his fellow workers. Many of those who had to work with him felt he had a superior attitude and resented it. As a result, the department did not have the team spirit it otherwise would have had.

Jeff's supervisor gave a lot of thought to the problem and looked at it this way. Although Jeff was producing at the highest level in the department, the total productivity of the department had not gone up since he joined the group. Instead, it had gone down because he had done more damage (through his poor human relations) than he had done good (by his personal productivity). He was an outstanding employee when viewed alone; he was a poor employee when viewed as a member of a group.

A few weeks later, the supervisor was promoted to a more responsible position and management had to come up with a replacement. They decided to promote someone from within the department but they did not select Jeff. When he discovered he was not chosen, he demanded a full explanation from the personnel manager. He was told that he was the highest producer in the department but he was also the weakest person in human relations, and that management felt the other workers in the department would not respect him as a supervisor. The personnel director also made it clear to Jeff that in his opinion a person who could not be human relations smart before he became a supervisor would not be human relations smart after he became a supervisor.

Do you agree with the personnel manager's decision to pass over Jeff even though Jeff was the best producer? Give reasons why you agree or disagree. (For suggested answer, see page 201.)

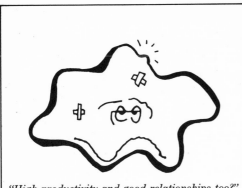

"High productivity and good relationships too?"

Success: Combining Productivity and Human Relations

There is a danger of misinterpretation in discussing human relations and productivity. It is conceivable that you might have deduced from the last few chapters that getting along with people (building strong and healthy vertical and horizontal working relationships) automatically results in greater departmental productivity. This is not necessarily true.

An employee can be happy, satisfied, and content with his job and yet not carry his fair share of the work load. A group of employees in a department can be getting along beautifully with each other, and yet the productivity of the department (in comparison with similar departments) might be far below average.

Happy employees are usually, but not always, high producers.

Therefore, the goal of good human relations is not just happy employees, *but happy employees that produce more.* The goal is greater productivity and ultimately a greater net profit. It is theoretically possible that a business organization could devote so much time and money to making employees happy and comfortable that the company could go broke and out of business. Management is therefore not interested in making people happy just because happy people are nice to have around or stick with their jobs longer. It is also interested in this because happy employees, under the right leadership, can be motivated to greater productivity.

This should not be interpreted to mean that employers are sensitive to the needs of their employees *only* because of greater productivity. This is not true. Nevertheless, management (and their employees) must fully accept the economic truth that survival under free competition requires a continual improvement in personal and group productivity. If product prices are to remain stable, increases in wages, greater fringe benefits, better working conditions, and improved physical facilities are possible only when there is an increase in productivity to accompany them.

The employee who is fun to be around but never gets down to doing his share of the work is a burden to his fellow workers. The nice guy who puts up a beautiful smoke screen of good human relations but seldom gets his assigned work out is a parasite on the productivity of others. He may be pleasant to have around, but he is far too expensive for management to keep.

The work itself must be done.

Labor costs must be controlled.

Customers must be well served.

Greater productivity must be the goal of American business organizations if they are to survive and compete with other world markets where labor costs are much lower. The development and use of more and more highly technical equipment (automation) will take us a long way, but personal productivity must do the rest.

It is only natural, then, that management should seek outstanding people for jobs that are increasingly sophisticated.

attitude should be directed by employer also. where is all their smarts.

It is only natural that they should try to find, employ, and train people who are sensitive to various human factors.

What are these human factors? The best way to introduce the most important one is to present another hypothetical situation.

This time we will assume that there is a small department with one male supervisor and three female employees. All three of these women have identical assignments and similar work loads. We will further assume that Alice and Hazel have been employed in their positions for one year. Marilyn, on the other hand, joined the organization yesterday as a replacement for an employee who resigned. Marilyn is ten years younger than Alice or Hazel. She has a very high potential that is substantially above that of either of the other two women. She is also very pretty.

Alice and Hazel have been taking it very easy in the department, and there has been a sizable gap between their current level of productivity and their potentials. In other words, they have not been motivated to do the kind of job they can do. Marilyn is very ambitious. She wants to build a reputation for herself and, if possible, move quickly to a supervisory position where she will have more responsibility and remuneration. She does not want to stand still, *so she already has one of the most important plus factors management seeks.* In order to move ahead, Marilyn has decided that it will be necessary for her to increase her personal level of productivity to the point where it will be above that of Alice and Hazel.

She has also decided that she can do this in either of two ways. First, she could go about it very quickly. She could pour on the steam and pass Alice and Hazel in a hurry, but in using this approach she could pay only a little attention to building good horizontal working relationships with them. Second, she could pass Alice and Hazel in personal productivity on a much slower schedule, so that at the same time she could concentrate on building good horizontal relationships with them in an attempt to increase *their* productivity along with her own.

What might happen if Marilyn decided to follow the first approach and ignore building relationships?

It is possible, of course, that Alice and Hazel might be

motivated (perhaps in order to make their positions more secure) to compete with Marilyn, and as a result the productivity of the entire department might increase.

It is also possible that many unfortunate things could happen. For example, Alice and Hazel might resent Marilyn, and rather than work with her they could, in subtle ways, work against her. Because they are more experienced, they might let her make some mistakes that they could prevent if they wanted to. They could do many little things that would make her uncomfortable and her work more difficult. As a result, she might become critical of Alice and Hazel, and the relationships between the three could deteriorate to a point where the productivity of all three would drop. This would be especially obvious if customers were involved.

This might not happen, of course. But it could happen! And if it did, Marilyn would certainly not have helped her future with the company. It is not a safe approach for her to take. She could be asking for trouble.

Now what might happen if Marilyn took the opposite approach—if she passed Alice and Hazel in personal productivity very slowly but at the same time worked hard to build good, strong working relationships with them?

It is likely that Marilyn would make her job easier. She would be valued more by the supervisor. She would earn the support of both Alice and Hazel. She would contribute more to productivity. Instead of falling into a human relations trap, she would demonstrate to management that she has insight and sensitivity.

Of course it would be easy to tell Marilyn that building good working relationships with Alice and Hazel is the best route to take. But how should she go about doing it? Here are six simple suggestions that should help.

1. Marilyn would be smart to go about increasing her personal productivity gradually so that it would not be noticeable to Alice, Hazel, or to the supervisor. If she made an all-out effort to overtake Alice and Hazel, she could put them in a bad light with the supervisor and cause resentment that would hurt everyone involved.

2. Marilyn could build better horizontal relationships with the two older women if she would sacrifice a little of

her personal productivity to help increase theirs. She could accomplish this by looking for opportunities to help Alice and Hazel when their work load is heavy or when they do not feel well. She could even pitch in and clean up extra work they have been assigned, should either one be absent.

3. As Marilyn brings her personal productivity above that of Alice and Hazel, she should be careful not to become critical of them because their performance levels are now lower than hers. She must not expect any great ego satisfaction or continual praise from her supervisor just because she is, at this point in her career, carrying a larger share of the work load.

4. Marilyn should be careful not to isolate herself too much from Alice and Hazel during breaks, lunch periods, and other times of inactivity. Even if she is occasionally rejected by them, she must continue to be pleasant until good relationships are built. She must be sincerely interested in both Alice and Hazel as individuals in order to win their respect. A superior attitude on her part will defeat any effort she makes to build sound relationships.

5. She should not, under any circumstances, take advantage of her attractiveness to play up to the supervisor. In fact, she should build her relationship with the supervisor upon her personal productivity and human relations ability *only*. Any other approach will do far more harm than good.

6. Above all, Marilyn should stand on her own two feet and work out her own problems without complaining or running to the supervisor for help. She can only achieve the respect of Alice and Hazel by demonstrating to them that she knows what she is doing and can fight her own battles.

Marilyn will go a long way in communicating to management that she has one of the *human relations plus factors* they seek if she keeps the following principle in mind: *An increase in personal productivity should be accompanied by increased attention to horizontal relationships.*

You might feel that all of this is expecting too much of Marilyn or of any new employee who is ambitious and wishes to improve his position with his organization. Perhaps. But doesn't it really depend on how important personal progress is to the individual? If Marilyn were to jog along with Alice and Hazel, she would not of course be sufficiently motivated to give such a plus factor to her job. But since she wishes to qualify for better opportunities, it is a price she must be willing to pay. Personal productivity is only one of many plus factors, and it is not enough to take Marilyn as far as she wishes to go. She must also be very human relations smart.

Last week Marilyn was invited to have a long talk with the personnel director of her company. During the conversation she asked what kind of a person management was really seeking? The personnel director said that, in his opinion, management usually looks for four plus factors in employees they hope to promote into management. Marilyn made a big effort to remember all four, and this is the way she would probably put it now should you ask her.

1. The person management is looking for strives to work close to his personal potential regardless of the level at which his fellow workers are performing. He is always trying to close his personal productivity gap even though others are content to do only what they have to in order to keep their jobs. He is self-motivating. He is not satisfied to drag along. He abhors mediocrity in a person who has a high potential. He takes a professional approach to his job and gains great satisfaction when he does it well.

2. He is never really satisfied with his personal potential. He believes that he can always improve it a little. He truly believes in lifelong learning. He takes advantage of any training that the company will provide. He continues to read and study on his own. He is always learning more and more about the job ahead of him. He may even continue his formal education by attending classes at a nearby adult education center, junior or senior college, or university. Although he is realistic about his potential, he does not agree with some who say it cannot be improved. He does not go along with the concept that a person is born with a certain potential that cannot be changed. He will continue to learn and to prepare for new opportunities.

To put it another way, he refuses to put his potential on the shelf. He wants to raise it higher and higher, so that he will be ready for future opportunities. He does not resent others who have higher potentials; he simply wants to make the most of his own.

3.   He doesn't feel that human relations is a lot of foolishness. He puts people ahead of machines, statistics, procedures, and credentials. He accepts the responsibility of building strong relationships as an interesting and inevitable challenge. He is highly productive, and at the same time he protects his relationships with people. He does this with a sense of humor and personal understanding. He is proud of the fact that he is a good person to work next to. He doesn't overplay his hand by becoming mushy or flowery in his approach to others; he endeavors to keep all relations on a sincere level. He does all of this because he knows that he contributes to the productivity of his department in two ways: one, through his own personal work effort; and two, through the relationships he builds with his fellow employees. He refuses to sacrifice one for the other, and he constantly tries to keep them in proper balance.

He refuses to be a mediocre employee, and yet the knowledge that others will settle for less doesn't upset him. He refuses to let group pressures make an average employee out of him, and yet he will not permit such attitudes to isolate him from others. He keeps his own identity and still works well with the group. He doesn't let petty human problems destroy his effectiveness. In short, he works at human relations and is not ashamed to let anybody know it.

4.   He makes a point of being loyal to his company or organization. This does not mean that he automatically accepts all of the policies and practices that filter down from the top. Far from it. He accepts the responsibility of making changes, but he remains loyal to his company while he fights to bring such changes about. He feels that his company deserves his best effort, and should the day come when this is no longer possible he will be honest with himself (and the company) and resign. He simply refuses to work for any organization unless he can be positive about it ninety-five percent of the time. He refuses to let human relations problems, the negative attitudes of others, or personal disappointments slow him down. He sets goals for himself, but if he does not reach

his goals according to his own time schedule, he does not become overly disturbed. He knows that he will probably accomplish his life's work inside an organizational framework, so he studies things carefully and tries to be patient and see the whole picture.

Marilyn asked the personnel director a second question: "How many employees will I find in your company that have all of the four plus factors?"

He replied: "It is impossible to say. There are many who are good at one or two, some who are good at three, but only a very few who are good at all four. At any rate, those who demonstrate all four do not remain line employees for long, unless by choice, because they are desperately needed for supervisory positions."

Marilyn then followed with her last question: "How does management single out those who have the plus factors they seek?"

"It's very easy," replied the director. "You only have to be slightly taller than others to stand out in a crowd, and it is the same with the plus factors. You don't have to be miles ahead of others for management to recognize you; a little is all it takes."

Yes, the challenge is there for those who are ambitious and wish to accept it, and those who do accept it will find their personal progress substantial. It is something to think seriously about!

PROBLEM

6

The Unhappy High Producer

Ted walked in the back door, grunted in a negative manner to his wife, and sat down at the kitchen table. It took Ted some time to express his exasperation. Here is a summary of his story.

Ted had been with the Kramer Corporation for more than nine months. From his first day, he had been determined to set a pace that would bring him advancement. It took him a little while to catch on to the job, but within four months he was up to the average of others in productivity. After a few more months he was the top producer in the department. In the meantime, the others maintained a steady, but slower, pace.

Ted felt good about his ability to pass others in the department, but he was disturbed because he had received no recognition for the achievement. In fact, the harder he worked, the more difficult it was to get along with the others. Even the supervisor had failed to give Ted any encouragement. After a few weeks of being the top producer, Ted became more critical of the others; he started to give out a few tips on how they might improve their efficiency, and he began to sound off more in staff meetings.

The whole situation had reached a boiling point today when Ted was strongly counseled by his supervisor to be more patient and understanding with his fellow workers. "Look Ted," said his supervisor, "you've got it all going for you, but you will never win a promotion if you blow your cool with your fellow employees. Slow down a little. You have a very high potential and your productivity is great, but you can't expect others to equal your pace. I don't want you to destroy now the very relationships you might have to rebuild later should you take my place."

Was Ted's exasperation justified? Or did his supervisor have a good point? (For suggested answer, see page 202.)

"Yes, sir, I understand my supervisor perfectly."

Your Most Important Working Relationship

The most important working relationship you must deal with is the one between you and your immediate supervisor. This single relationship can speed up your personal progress or slow it down to a discouraging crawl; it can make going to work a joy or a drag; it can prepare you for greater responsibilities or it can frustrate your desire to learn. And there is just no way to avoid the human relations fact that your supervisor is a VIP—a Very Important Person—who, good or bad, you must learn to cope with.

What kind of a person will you draw as a supervisor?

It is impossible to predict. However, he will be basically the same person he used to be when he held a job similar to yours, except that now he has much more responsibility.

He may or may not have been given some special training to help him become a good supervisor. He may be easy to get along with, or he may be very difficult. He may be sensitive to your needs, or he may be insensitive. He may be feeling his way along and making many mistakes, or he may be highly experienced and a real pro at his job. The one thing you can depend on is the fact that he won't be like any person you have ever had to get along with before. This is true for three reasons: (1) he probably has a strong personality that gave him the confidence to become a supervisor in the first place; (2) the responsibilities of being a supervisor probably weigh heavily on his shoulders; (3) he has work authority over you, which makes him different from any other authority figure you may have known in the past.

What is a supervisor? A supervisor is many things.

He is a *teacher*. He will not only teach you the routine of your new job, but he will also have a great influence on your attitude toward your job and the company. He has a reservoir of knowledge, skills, and techniques that you need to learn. You will be most fortunate if he is a good teacher. If he is not, you will have to learn from observation.

He is a *counselor*. His job is to see that you live up to your potential. He might need to correct errors you are making. He may need to give you tips on improving yourself as an employee. He may feel the need to have a heart-to-heart talk with you at times.

He is a *leader*. More than anything else, your supervisor must provide the leadership your department requires. He must see that you are happy and productive, but he cannot neglect others in the department. He must provide motivation for all employees. He must earn your respect not by being soft and easy, but by being a strong leader who will help you build a long-range career.

It would be a mistake to attempt to *type* supervisors. They cannot be clearly classified into different groups. Each supervisor has a unique personality. He will operate under his own system just as your teachers did.

Do you recall your early school days when you discovered the differences between teachers? You may have had one who expected a great deal more from you than others did.

At the time you may not have liked this person, yet, years later, he or she may have become your favorite. The same can be true with supervisors.

When you start a new job you don't want an easygoing supervisor who does not care and, as a result, will hurt instead of help your future. You will be better off with a more concerned, more demanding supervisor who will help you reach your potential. With an easy supervisor you might develop some poor working habits and eventually become unhappy with yourself. With a stronger supervisor, one who will take time to train you, you will become a better worker and improve your future. But no matter what kind of a boss you bump into, it is up to you to learn to understand him and work efficiently under his kind of leadership.

You must do some of the adjusting.

You must provide some of the understanding.

You must help in building the relationship that must exist between the two of you.

Each individual supervisor creates his own special climate, or atmosphere, under which you must operate. The following analysis of three kinds of climates may give you some indication of the adjustments you might have to make in the future.

The Structured Climate

Some supervisors are more strict than others. They operate a very tight department by keeping very close, and sometimes restrictive, controls. They frequently expect employees to be precisely on time, orderly, and highly efficient. They permit foolishness only when a very special occasion calls for it. Ninety-eight percent of the time they stick strictly to business.

The supervisor who creates this kind of atmosphere often appears cold, distant, and unfeeling to the new employee. He seems unreachable. He seems unreasonable. As a result, the new employee may begin to fear him.

Two things might help you if you find yourself working for a supervisor who creates this kind of climate. (1) Some jobs force supervisors to be more autocratic than do others.

Some kinds of work require a very high level of efficiency. For example, a supervisor of telephone operators might, of necessity, have to be autocratic in order to maintain the level of split-second efficiency that this job requires. Work of a highly technical nature in which certain precision standards must be met will call for a different climate than work that is primarily in a service field. In other words, the work to be done often has more to do with the climate than the supervisor does. (2) Although the supervisor who establishes this kind of atmosphere may appear cold and unapproachable, the direct opposite may be true. He is probably more interested in you and more willing to help you than you suspect. One must not be afraid of a supervisor of this kind. It may take more time to build a meaningful relationship with him, but once achieved, it might be more valuable. Adjusting to a structured or autocratic climate is not easy for many young workers, especially when one has not been exposed to it previously.

The Permissive Climate

The direct opposite of the structured climate is the permissive atmosphere. Some supervisors are very free and easy in creating a working climate. They provide little or no direct leadership. There is an absence of intervention. It is a loose situation with few controls or restrictions.

This permissive climate can be the most dangerous of all for the new employee, because the need for self-discipline on his part is so great. Because he does not feel the presence of a leader, he may not make good use of his time; because he is given very little encouragement, he may find it difficult to motivate himself; because things are so easygoing, he may relax too much and become too friendly with fellow workers. All of this can cause bad habits that can lead to mutual dissatisfaction. Instead of being an ideal climate, it becomes a trap that destroys the desire to succeed and eventually causes great unhappiness.

Whether we like to accept it or not, strong but sensitive leadership gives us more job security and forces us to live closer to our potential. In most cases, a little too much may be better than very little. Beware of a climate that is too relaxed unless you are a self-starter and you can discipline yourself. You might discover that too much freedom is your downfall.

The Democratic Climate

The goal of most supervisors in modern organizations is to create a democratic climate. This atmosphere is the most difficult of all to establish. In fact, just as it is true in all of our American institutions, purely democratic action is often a goal rather than a reality.

A democratic climate is one in which the employees *want* to do what the supervisor wants done. The supervisor becomes one of the group and still retains his leadership role. He permits the employees to have a great deal to say about the operation of the department. Everyone becomes involved, because each person works from inside the group rather than from outside. The supervisor is the leader and a member of the group at the same time, and as a result a team feeling is created. Many isolated cases of research indicate that most people will respond with greater personal satisfaction and greater productivity if the supervisor can achieve and maintain a democratic atmosphere.

If this is true, why can't more supervisors create and maintain this kind of climate? There are many reasons.

In the first place, it is the most difficult to create, and once it is created it is far more difficult to maintain. It requires a real expert, an individual with great skill and sensitivity; one should not expect to find a great number of supervisors with this ability.

In the second place, not all workers will respond to this climate, ideal as it may seem. *You* may like it best, but others in your department may like a more autocratic approach. This is especially true when there are younger workers in a department where many more experienced and older employees work. You will often hear employees say: "I wish he would quit fooling around and *tell* us what to do"; "I wish he would tighten up things around here—those people are getting away with murder"; "He is too easy. I can't enjoy working for someone who doesn't set things down clearly and specifically from the beginning."

In the third place, the supervisor who aspires to build a true democratic climate always finds himself somewhere between the structured and the permissive. He may approach the ideal situation for awhile, only to find that a few employees are taking advantage of him. When this happens it is necessary to tighten up again and become more structured.

In recent years, a great deal of attention has been given by those in management to what is called Theory X and Theory Y in leadership styles. Theory X represents management by control, and states that the worker must be directed, motivated, and controlled in order to achieve high productivity. Theory Y represents participative management, and states that the worker will achieve greater productivity if he can set his own goals and direct his own efforts through involvement. The interested reader can explore this concept in detail by reading *The Human Side of Enterprize* by Professor Douglas M. McGregor. The point to be made here is that one supervisor may lean towards Theory X while another may try to put Theory Y into practice, so the worker must be prepared to work under either or both.

Every supervisor creates his own individual climate. Some supervisors come up with a workable blend of the structured and democratic; others come up with a blend of the permissive and democratic; still others have a special blend that is all their own. We call this their *leadership style*.

Whether we personally like a supervisor or his style is not as important as whether we can learn to be productive in the climate he creates. The new worker should not be too quick to judge, however, because it is often true that what appears to be a difficult climate at the beginning might turn out to be a comfortable and beneficial one later on. For example, one of the best things your supervisor can do is to go to bat for you with upper management. The communication that takes place between your supervisor and management concerning you and your progress is often the key to your future success. It is quite possible that a supervisor will expect a great deal from you, criticize you, even make you unhappy at times, and then, when the chips are down, be the first to go to bat for you.

It is always good to remember that your supervisor also has a boss and sometimes he must be more demanding than he wishes because of instructions from above. Your supervisor may be under more pressure than you suspect, and although he may try to absorb it to protect you, he may not always be successful.

So what kind of a supervisor might you run into on your first assignment?

Hopefully you will draw a sensitive supervisor who can create a comfortable climate and provide the right amount of leadership to meet your needs and help you reach your full potential. Chances are fairly good this will happen, but don't bank on it. As a matter of cold reality, something quite different could occur.

Pam, for example, started her career working for a supervisor who made a play for her. She had to fight him off for days until he finally got the message, reversed himself, and started treating her the way he should have at the beginning. It was a difficult period for Pam, and only because she stood her ground forcefully and openly was she able to live through it and keep her positive attitude.

Roberto discovered rather quickly that his boss was frequently drunk on the job and management either did not know about it or chose to overlook it. Some days Roberto and his fellow workers took a great deal of abuse. On other days the supervisor disappeared for long periods, and they had to get the work out without his help. All of this caused Roberto to take a very critical view of all supervisors, but fortunately this supervisor was eventually transferred to another department and his replacement was so good that Roberto's faith was soon restored.

Perhaps Ryan's first supervisor was even more difficult to deal with than the two cited above. This one played one employee against the other so that nobody in the department knew where he stood. He would have a favorite for a few days and then, without provocation, reject this person and switch to another. Finally it became obvious to management that productivity was in a nosedive and would not improve, and they took action. The new supervisor was everything Ryan could have wanted, but it took him a long time to forget his first unfortunate experience.

The above examples, to be sure, are not typical. Most supervisors are sensitive, sincere, and serious people who will do their best to build a strong, healthy relationship with you. But whether you draw a good, bad, or indifferent supervisor, it will be your responsibility to build the best possible relationship with him or her. To help you meet this challenge, here are ten tips that should help you.

1. *Don't transfer early negative attitudes you may have had towards other authority figures in your life to your supervisor.* Some young people who have had problems with parents, older brothers and sisters, teachers, police, and similar authority figures make the foolish mistake of transferring their feelings of hostility to their first supervisor, simply because he represents another authority figure. This is grossly unfair to the supervisor and is the worst possible way to get started on a new job. Wipe away any previous negative feelings you may have and give your new boss a free, open, honest, and unprejudiced opportunity to build a healthy relationship with you. His role is much different from that of other authority figures because he is primarily interested in your on-the-job performance. If you give him a fair chance, he will almost always earn your respect instead of your hostility.

2. *Whenever possible, take the positive approach and try to make your supervisor look good.* Except under rare circumstances where the behavior of your supervisor does not deserve it, you will be smart to make your supervisor look good, because your success, to some extent, depends upon his. Indirectly, when you put him in a good light you automatically help yourself. For example, if your boss receives a promotion, two things might happen to you: (1) if you are the best available candidate, you might be promoted to his job; (2) he might go to bat for you from his new and more strategic position. Normally speaking, if you have the right relationship with your supervisor, the more successful he becomes the more chance you will have to advance.

3. *Expect some rough days under his supervision.* Everyone, including supervisors, is entitled to a few bad days. Your boss is only human. If he should boil over on a given day, don't let it throw you. If he seems to be picking on you for a while, give him time to get over it. More important than anything else, try not to take personally anything he does that you don't like. There may be times when you do not understand the behavior of your boss, but if you can float along with it, chances are good that it won't last long.

4. *Don't nurse a small gripe into a major issue.* A small gripe, when nurtured, can get blown up all out of proportion and can lead to a confrontation with your supervisor that will hurt your relationship. If you have a legitimate gripe, try to talk it over with him quickly so that you can get it out of your system before it builds up. It will take some initiative on your part to do this, and you must be sensitive enough to select the right time; but it is the best posture to take. Remember: he won't know you have a complaint unless you tell him.

5. *Select the right time to approach your supervisor.* Whether you have a complaint or a positive suggestion to make, try to approach your supervisor at the right time. He may be too busy or under too much pressure on a given day to talk to you. If so, wait it out. When the pressure is off, chances are good he will give you a fair opportunity. However, if you do make a mistake and try to talk to him at the wrong time, and if he abruptly turns you off, wait until another day and try again. If it is important to you, he will no doubt want to talk to you about it. Give him another chance.

6. *Never go above your supervisor's head without talking to him first.* The easiest and quickest way to destroy your relationship with your supervisor is to go over his head on a problem that involves him or his department. Always talk to him first. If you do not receive what you feel to be adequate satisfaction, you can then take other action. At least this way he will know that you consulted him first.

7. *Don't let your supervisor intimidate you.* Fear is a strong emotion. If you are so fearful of your boss that you cannot approach him, you should talk to personnel, consider a possible transfer, or if necessary resign. You will never be happy

working for a person you fear, and a supervisor will never respect you if you are afraid of him.

8. *Don't try to make a buddy of your supervisor.* Your relationship with your supervisor is a business relationship. Keep it that way. The distance between you and your boss may often appear to be a fine line, but he is still your boss. If you get too personal, it will almost always turn out badly.

9. *Don't be afraid to apologize to your supervisor when you make a mistake.* Everyone makes mistakes, so if you make a serious goof and injure your relationship with your boss, why not clean the slate with an honest apology? It is a good idea to leave work every day with a pleasant feeling toward your job and your supervisor. If you have had trouble with him on a given day and in all honesty realize that some of the fault is yours, the mature thing to do is accept your share of the blame. You will feel better and so will your supervisor.

10. *Remember that not all supervisors are in love with their roles.* A surprising number of those who are supervisors would really prefer to be workers, but they have accepted such responsibility because they feel they can contribute more as a supervisor or because they can make more money. If, as an employee, you view this as a possibility, it will give you more insight into the role itself and perhaps give you more tolerance and understanding. Try to remember that for the great majority of people, being a good supervisor is a very difficult thing, and sometimes those that try the hardest to win the respect of their workers never fully succeed because of personality traits they cannot change.

In summary, building and maintaining a strong, warm, productive relationship with your boss is a real human relations challenge. It isn't always easy. Yet it is an essential step in your progress. You may get used to one supervisor only to discover that you have been transferred to another department and have to start from scratch. Every relationship will be a unique challenge. Make the most of every experience.

PROBLEM

7

A Choice in Supervisors

Suppose you are a career employee with a large utility company. For the last sixty days you have been on a training program preparing for a new position and assignment. You have just received word to report to the personnel department to discuss your new role in the company.

The personnel director gives you a choice of assignments. He tells you that two departments have requested your services. The departments are identical in their operations. The basic difference is the supervisor himself and the type of climate he creates in his department. You have had a chance to observe both.

One department has a rather demanding supervisor who leans in the direction of Theory X. He believes in rather rigid performance standards and controls. He is an old-timer and has been in charge of his department for many years. He expects and receives high productivity and loyalty from all his employees. Everyone admits that he has trained more people who are now in top management positions than anyone in the company.

The other department is run by a younger supervisor who adheres as far as possible to Theory Y. He tries to get everyone in the department to participate in decisions and get involved. He prides himself on his democratic approach and feels he has been very successful. People appear very happy working for him. The personnel turnover is less in this department than in the other. Productivity is almost, but not quite, as high.

Which department would you select? On what basis? (For suggested answer, see page 203.)

"You can't build perfect relationships with everybody."

Relationship Overtones

The purpose of this chapter is to look more deeply into the nature of working relationships. To do this we will explore six different characteristics that are often involved. These characteristics or elements can have a considerable influence on the quality or tone of the relationship. In a sense, they constitute the ingredients or components that make up the relationship itself.

Although it is an admitted oversimplification, perhaps you will understand the whole idea of a relationship better if you visualize it as an invisible tunnel between two fellow employees. The following illustration will give you the picture.

The two-way arrows (between the amoebas) remind us that verbal communication is the lifeblood of the relationship and

that frequent conversation is vital if the relationship is to remain active and healthy. Good input and good receiving are necessary from those at both ends. The illustration below adds to the relationship those factors we will deal with in this chapter.

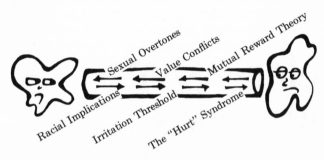

Of course, not all of the above characteristics or elements are likely to be present in any single relationship. Some relationships may have only one or two of them. Others may have four or five. An investigation of each of the above, however, will give you additional insight into the nature of all working relationships.

Sexual overtones: It goes without saying that working relationships between members of the opposite sex almost always have sexual overtones. If you are a man, you will recognize and build a relationship with a woman in a different way than if she were a man. You might tease her differently, use different language, and perhaps play the role of the gentleman in your contacts with her. If the woman happens to be your supervisor, you should be careful not to let your male pride prevent you from seeing that many women make excellent managers. If you are a woman, you will recognize and build a relationship with a man in a much different manner. For example, you might decide to be more distant so that there is no danger of others accusing you of flirting to gain special advantages. If the man (be he your supervisor or a fellow employee) makes continual plays for you, you should be polite but firm in maintaining a business-only relationship. The great majority of men and women work together without any serious complications arising because of sex. The overtones remain subdued and have no adverse influence on productivity. But not always. Take the case of Judy.

Judy was attracted sexually to her supervisor from the moment he was transferred into her department. A perceptive observer would have noticed that the very next day she started wearing the best clothes in her wardrobe; she became more particular with her makeup; she started working harder to win the favor of her new boss and to create more opportunities to talk with him on business matters. So what happened? The other women in Judy's department quickly sensed the sexual overtones to the relationship and their relationship toward Judy began to cool off in a hurry. They became more distant, less willing to help her, and less tolerant of her mistakes. It didn't take long for a certain strain to develop among all employees in the department, and productivity began to suffer.

The case of Judy raises a very difficult question: *What are the human relations dangers involved in dating someone where you work?*

There is little danger involved providing the individual is not your supervisor, he or she works in a section separated from yours, and you are smart enough to keep your business and personal worlds apart. Under these circumstances, management will probably be very understanding. After all, it is only normal and healthy for people of the opposite sex to be attracted to each other because of on-the-job contacts. Management cannot keep this from happening. There are some real dangers, however, that you should know about in advance. Most of them occur under the following circumstances: (1) when a supervisor dates someone in his or her own department, thus raising immediate cries of favoritism and hurting productivity; (2) when two people, especially if they are in the same section, date and do not keep their business and personal worlds separated, thus hurting relationships with others and eventually lowering productivity; (3) when one or both parties are married, thus creating a sticky situation that can produce harmful gossip, hurt productivity, and sometimes make it necessary for management to step in.

Before you create or accept a dating situation where you work, you should also consider the chance of a breakup between the two of you at a later date that might leave hard feelings among fellow employees who were in on the matter and might have taken sides. Another point to keep in mind is the action you would take should the dating become serious and marriage plans evolve. In cases of this nature, it would be a good human relations move on your part to announce the decision to management personally before it gets into the grapevine and they find out about it secondhand. Management appreciates receiving such important information directly, and within the framework of written policy, they can be very accommodating.

Racial implications: The most important of all human relations principles is to respect and treat every person as a unique and special individual. Look beyond outward physical appearances, ignore how he or she might resemble someone you have had an unfavorable experience with in the past, and accept each person for himself alone. If everybody could sincerely adhere to this one fundamental practice, relationships would have a good chance of functioning harmoniously. Each person—and each relationship—would stand on its own without reference to color, race, creed, or sex. Unfortunately for all of us, not enough people practice this principle. Here are two short cases to illustrate the point.

Although he had always thought he was free of prejudice, Jack had had very little close contact with blacks. He was, therefore, a little uneasy about working closely with one for the first time. Hobart, a young black, joined the department and, after introductions, Jack's uneasiness gave way to anticipation. Hobart was a very easy-to-know, friendly guy. He would be fun to work with. Everything went very well

as far as their relationship was concerned until Hobart started to make a number of mistakes. He kept asking what Jack
felt were a bunch of stupid questions, and, in general, he
did not live up to Jack's expectations. Jack became so frustrated over the matter that he was tempted to go to his
supervisor. Then, all of a sudden, it came to him that he
was expecting more of Hobart because he was black. He was
looking for things to complain about instead of being understanding like he would normally be with a white person. Jack
decided to get the relationship back on a fair footing, so he
invited Hobart for coffee and admitted his mistake. It was
a good move because Hobart had felt Jack's negative attitude
and wanted to build a better relationship himself.

Fernando and Archie were assigned two months ago as a
team on a moving van for a large company that operated
inside the geographical limits of a large city. Archie had graduated from a community college and hoped to eventually
get into management; Fernando, a very sensitive Chicano,
was a high school drop-out with over three years experience
in the furniture-moving business.

Archie learned quickly that Fernando was an outstanding
worker with excellent skills. He also learned in a hurry that
Fernando was not much of a talker. In fact, Fernando only
communicated when it was necessary to get the job done.
This silence quickly got on Archie's nerves and, after making
many attempts to get a light conversation going, he decided
that Fernando had a lot of deep-seated hostility towards
Anglos. It was a very uncomfortable situation, and because
Archie needed to talk, he soon became a little bitter about
the situation. Should he ask for a transfer? Should he resign?
Then one day it occurred to him that with a few beers Fernando might open up and they could learn to communicate. He
invited Fernando to be his guest, and they went to a place
close to Fernando's home. It was a small place that reflected
the Chicano culture. Sure enough, it wasn't long before Fernando felt sufficiently comfortable to start talking. Archie
learned a great deal. Fernando had been pushed around by
many people. He did not feel accepted. His silence was more
a defense than anything else. But what got to Archie was
the fact that Fernando felt that Archie was against *him*, and

not the other way around. It was a revelation for both parties, and much of the tension that was present on the job previously was gone the next day. Archie and Fernando learned how to communicate, and, as a result, they worked much better as a team. They didn't become personal friends, but they gained a high degree of mutual toleration.

There are many relationships ahead of you that will have certain racial implications. They will not always be easy to understand. Sometimes they may demand more perception than you possess. Yet, if you are open, honest, sincere, and willing to talk, your chances of building sound relationships are excellent.

Irritation threshold: Relationships are frequently endangered because one of the individuals has an irritating habit or mannerism that bothers the other. Here are some of the most common ones:

Harsh, overbearing voices
Irritating laughs
Constant name dropping
Always talking about money
Constant reference to sex
Telling dirty or unfunny stories
Overuse of certain words or expressions
Constant discussion of personal problems
Constant complaining
Always bragging about success

Whether or not a habit or mannerism becomes an irritant depends upon the threshold or *tolerance level* of the second party. If one party has a high enough threshold he may not even notice an irritant that might bother someone else. On the other hand, it is possible for an individual to have a very low threshold to a certain mannerism, in which case the habit can do considerable damage to the relationship.

Diane is an excellent example of a young employee who hurt her relationship with a few fellow workers because of a nervous giggle that followed almost every sentence she uttered. Obviously Diane had no idea what was happening. She was not conscious of the habit or the fact that it was hurting her relationships with certain people who had low thresholds. One day, after getting a complaint from a good employee who worked next to Diane, the supervisor had a talk with her about it and, thanks to some very hard work on Diane's part, the irritating mannerism largely disappeared in a few weeks.

Although once the individual knows about them bad habits can be modified or sometimes eliminated, the person at the other end of the relationship must not expect too much too soon. In some cases it may be necessary to learn to live with certain irritants by making an attempt to raise one's threshold or tolerance level. Seldom do such irritants come from only one side of the relationship. Almost all of us have at least a few mannerisms or habits that bother other people. The individual, even in the business environment, retains the right to remain pretty much the way he is, so some adjustment on your part to such factors will be necessary in most relationships.

Mutual reward theory: With proper care and cultivation, working relationships can turn out to be mutually rewarding and both parties can come out ahead. In fact, it is easy to build a case for the fact that if a working relationship is to remain healthy over a long period of time, it must contribute something of value to both persons. The case of Kate and Janet illustrates the theory.

Kate was a very quiet, conservative, serious worker with outstanding job knowledge. Janet, on the other hand, was a very popular, socially outgoing person with limited job knowledge. They worked next to each other in identical jobs and, despite their differences, they slowly built a strong and mutually rewarding relationship. How did it happen? Kate made a great effort to teach Janet as much as possible about the job and took care of some mistakes Janet made without the supervisor finding out about them. What did Janet do in return? She helped Kate build more social confidence in herself by advising her on what to wear, by improving her makeup, and by introducing her to some of her friends. Because both parties contributed to the success of the other, their relationship became a strong one and the productivity of both parties increased.

Relationships can almost always be mutually rewarding because people can strengthen each other in many different ways. Obviously, however, when one person does all the giving, deterioration quickly sets in. As you build new relationships and protect old ones, look for things you can do to contribute to the success and happiness of the person next to you. When you do this you will almost always receive something in return that will make life better for you.

Value conflicts: Everyone has his own value system. Everyone has his own priority list as far as what is really important in life. Different people seek different life styles. Because of this, it is only natural that value conflicts exist between people who have been forced to associate with each other closely in the world of work. Here are two typical examples.

Tony was assigned to work next to Mr. Henderson who was more than twice his age. Tony was a bachelor who liked an active social life and did not want to assume family responsibilities too soon in life. His fancy foreign sports car and fashionable clothing reflected his attitude. He was determined to come up with a life style different from that of his parents. Mr. Henderson, on the other hand, was a very traditional, highly family-oriented, and religious person. How did they learn to work together gracefully? At the beginning they both played it cool and built their relationship exclusively on job factors. Tony learned to respect Mr. Henderson for his many years of job experience and his willingness to share it. Mr. Henderson learned to respect Tony for his willingness to learn and contribute a full day's work. After six months they could even discuss their value differences. A better mutual understanding was brought about.

Beverley was brought up in a strict home environment and was taught to respect discipline. She was frequently considered square or straight by her contemporaries. Trish, on the other hand, was very happy-go-lucky and undisciplined. She considered herself very much ahead of others of her generation. How did Beverley and Trish get along when they were forced to work very closely with each other? At first the sparks of conflict were rather obvious. Slowly they built a sound working relationship based upon their mutual desire to do a good job for the company and further their careers. They did not become close personal friends, and they did not go out together socially; but they learned to respect each other and both benefited from the working relationship despite their value differences.

It is a mistake, perhaps even an invasion of privacy, to impose one's own personal values on another, especially in the working environment. What a fellow worker does with his life off-the-job is his own business and should have nothing to do with the relationship you build with him on-the-job. To react to an individual in a negative way on the inside for what he does on the outside is asking for trouble and should be avoided. There are, of course, always enough common interests on-the-job upon which to build a good and permanent working relationship. Look for these factors only. You will be surprised how many good working relationships you can build with people who think and live differently than you do.

The "hurt syndrome": There is a real danger that in building a worthwhile working relationship you might get your feelings hurt. All relationships are built on an emotional foundation. This being the case, people may expect more from a working relationship than they should, and consequently may wind up getting hurt. Here is a simple illustration of the point.

Mary and Sally joined the company the same day, and because they were thrown together during the orientation period, they became very close. For the first few weeks they spent all of their breaks together, isolated themselves from others during lunch, and became increasingly dependent upon each other. Unfortunately, Mary became over-dependent, and when Sally suddenly made the move to build relationships with others, Mary felt rejected and her feelings were hurt. It put a big strain on the working relationship for a few days. Then Sally, sensing Mary's reaction, initiated a long conversation about the matter. When Mary understood that Sally felt it was good human relations to build other relationships, and that she had not been snubbed, she felt better and decided to build some new working relationships herself.

Do those individuals who concentrate on building strong and healthy working relationships frequently live through a painful incident of some kind? The answer is yes. Many people make the mistake of trying to satisfy personal needs from a working relationship, when only a personal or social relationship can do it. In short, they expect too much from working relationships. Of course, it is difficult to build any relationship without occasional feelings of disappointment. We frequently expect more from the individual at the other end of the relationship than we should. Even those professionals who are highly successful at human relations must live through a few hurt feelings without magnifying them beyond their real dimensions. They must avoid pushing their disappointments with people underground where they fester and become distorted. Instead, they should discard them and continue to look for the healthy parts of the relationship. They must refuse to let the "hurt syndrome" destroy relationships that are basically sound and should be maintained.

As we conclude this chapter, there should be no doubt in the reader's mind about one thing: job relationships are intriguing, unpredictable, sometimes sticky, and, unlike personal and social relationships, are not freely chosen. They are sometimes hard to build in the first place, and they need constant attention to keep them healthy. Yet, despite all of this, they are fascinating and rewarding. As you move into the world of work on a career basis, you will have more and more opportunities to build strong and satisfying working relationships at all levels with all kinds of people.

PROBLEM

8

Molly Backs Away

Molly was an intelligent, sensitive college sophomore. She came from a very close Chicano family. Most people considered her to be very attractive. Molly had a job working part-time with a local banking organization and hoped to move into a good full-time career with the same company upon graduation in June.

Although she was fairly successful in her part-time job because she was reliable and conscientious, Molly did not make a big hit with her fellow workers because she had been taught that all relationships should be formal and impersonal. If she met a new girl on campus and the relationship began to get a little personal, she cut it off. When one of her fellow workers tried to be friendly, she was polite, but backed away. When someone tried to involve her in a discussion by asking a question, Molly came up with a quick answer but made no effort to keep the conversation going. A number of young men tried to date Molly without success.

Molly's supervisor, a perceptive man with many years of experience, said: "I have talked with Molly a number of times, and I am still at a loss as far as understanding her is concerned. She is a lovely person but she seems to be afraid to put even a little of herself into a relationship. I used to think it was just a matter of being shy and timid, but I'm not so sure anymore. Sometimes I sense a little hostility or defiance in her manner. Perhaps she is afraid she will be hurt. Perhaps she feels I am prejudiced against her. Perhaps it is just something about her culture I don't understand. At any rate, she doesn't seem to recognize that *she* has a responsibility to communicate. Until she learns this I cannot recommend her for a full-time position, because she will never make her full contribution to productivity."

What do you think of the supervisor's interpretation? (For suggested answer, see page 204.)

CHAPTER

"Hank's O.K. . . . he just needs motivation."

How to Compensate for Youth and Inexperience

The new employee who is young, capable, and ambitious is faced with a peculiar challenge in most organizations. And it doesn't take long for the challenge to present itself. You hear it expressed in many ways:

"I could have had that last promotion if I had had more seniority."

"Everyone in this outfit has age, seniority, or experience beyond mine. I'll never get a chance."

"I'm wasting my time and ability. I won't get a chance to show what I can do until I'm thirty."

"I think I'll grow a mustache, so that I'll at least appear older."

Many employees between the ages of eighteen and thirty

consider their youth a handicap. Some feel that they must put in time to reach a certain age level before they will be given a chance to demonstrate their ability. In a few cases the situation becomes aggravated because the employee appears younger than he is.

It is easy to appreciate this attitude if you put yourself in the place of the young employee. He sees older, more experienced employees all around him. He begins to feel that only time will compensate for the disadvantage of being young. He may even begin to feel the generation gap is wider inside a business organization than outside. Yet he wants to make progress. He wants to *move*. He doesn't want to wait. So the pressure builds.

Of course there is nothing wrong with being young and ambitious. There is nothing wrong with seeking more responsibility and opportunity. There is nothing wrong with wanting to make more money while you are still young and can enjoy spending it.

It is wrong, however, to dwell on a problem that can be overcome. While some young people dwell on the psychological disadvantages of their age and inexperience, *others set out to do something about it*. And we find many examples where they have been successful.

It is not unusual today to find young people in supervisory positions where some of the employees they supervise are many years their senior. Take Laurel and Leonard as examples.

Laurel manages a large fashion department, specializing in better clothing for mature women, in a major department store. She supervises nine full-time women, all of whom are old enough to be her mother. The department had sales of over $400,000 last year. The problems are constant and the pressure is great. How old is Laurel? She was twenty last month. Without exception, the older women consider her an excellent manager and her boss feels she has a great future.

Leonard, with only one year of college behind him, is the manager of a large, popular restaurant that is part of a major chain. Two of the three managers that work under him are much older than he, and one is old enough to be his father. As a matter of fact, most of the regular employees are older.

The establishment is open twenty-four hours a day, and the problems never stop. Yet Leonard seems to be on top of everything, and the president of the chain feels that he is just getting started. How old is Leonard? He'll be twenty-three next summer.

How do young people like Laurel and Leonard do it?

They demonstrate early that they can accept and handle responsibility; they demonstrate that they can make mature decisions; they demonstrate a great personal confidence. But more than anything else, they demonstrate a talent for human relations. *They show that they can build strong relationships with older and more experienced employees and management personnel.*

Young people who demonstrate these qualities have been largely responsible for the turnabout in some companies to an emphasis on youth and innovation rather than age and experience. Management in such companies has recognized in these young people a very promising combination of maturity, responsibility, initiative, and innovative ideas—ideas that help the company keep a young, up-to-date image. In other words, many young people have managed to turn a possible handicap into an asset.

However, all of the ambition, hard work, and good ideas you may have to offer a company won't help you advance unless you can build mature working relationships with others of all ages. You must look at it from management's point of view. How can you be considered for a position of leadership if you have not been able to win the respect and confidence of others regardless of age and experience? How can management move you ahead of older, more experienced people until you have shown that you have *already* built the right relationships with such people?

The fact is that your more mature fellow workers will not resist your personal progress if you go about it the right way. Rather, they will want you to succeed and will be willing to help you.

Your decision, then, is a simple one. If you are young and ambitious, you can either drift along until you are older and have more experience, or you can face the human relations problem now and speed up your progress.

If you decide to make the effort, there are a few important points to remember about building a relationship with an older, more experienced person.

First, remember that it is a matter of status to be successful and make progress on the job. For an older employee, to be passed up in favor of a younger person is difficult to take. Small wonder that the older, more experienced person may feel threatened by the younger man or women who is moving up in the organization.

Remember also that everyone, regardless of age, likes to be noticed. This is especially true of the more mature employee. They like to receive compliments (even if the compliments border on flattery). They like to feel that they are still important as employees and as people. They like to feel appreciated and respected.

Furthermore, it should be obvious that the more mature person often likes to keep a young image. Any action that tends to make this person feel out-of-touch or out-of-date is a mistake. Try to make him feel that he still has a lot to offer, that he is part of today's world, not yesterday's. Make a big effort to keep the communication lines open at all times. Do not isolate yourself from this person. Always include him in on fun and other activities. Remember, you cannot expect a good vertical relationship with him should you become his supervisor later on unless you build a good horizontal working relationship with him now.

Perhaps the most important aspect of building good relationships with mature fellow employees is your ability to earn *their* respect. This is done through ability, hard work, and reliability on a day-to-day basis.

There is no short, easy route. Deeds will do more than words. Statistics will do more than promises. Performance will do more than flattery.

Not that friendliness, personal interest, and concern for the more mature worker are unimportant. But personal interest will be second to performance in building a sound relationship.

More than anything else, *learn* from this person. His additional years of experience have taught him many things that you can learn without having to experience them. You can learn through osmosis, or absorption. Consider yourself an apprentice and learn. Then, if the time comes for you to move ahead of him, give him credit for making it possible. Let him have the satisfaction of calling you his protégé. Let him take pride in your success.

It will be smart of you to accept his role as an expert in areas where he is obviously better qualified than you.

It will be smart of you to keep your relationship on a formal basis until he gives you the signal to be more relaxed and personal.

It will be smart of you to see that he is always viewed by others in a good light.

Loyalty is a characteristic worth earning.

Look around you. There are many fine older men and women in every organization with many years of employment who take pride in helping young people advance. They have watched many hard workers climb right past them on the ladder to management. They have often been responsible for the push that made it possible.

Do not underestimate the influence of these people.

Many have the full respect of top management. Some have a direct line to important officials. They may not have your formal education, but they have made worthy contributions to the growth of the organization, and they have the respect of many people in all echelons.

Build your relationships with these people slowly. Give those with many years of service the respect due them. If you do this, then they in turn will give you the respect and support you need to succeed. They will look not at your age, but rather at your contribution. They will dwell not on your lack of experience, but rather on your potential. They will not count up your years of seniority, but rather they will count up your accomplishments.

If you are serious in wanting to build a career that will match your potential—and don't want to waste time doing it—you will find it necessary to concentrate on the relationships you build with mature fellow workers.

PROBLEM

9

A Challenge for Norman

Norman was a bright, energetic, forceful, and impatient young man who expected to earn an important management position by the time he was thirty and hoped to retire before he was fifty. Following graduation from a major university, he accepted a position with the R.K. Company for the following reasons: (1) the company was located near the beach where he and his wife had always dreamed of living; (2) the job gave him a good opportunity to learn more about all phases of the operation; (3) the salary was above average, and the side benefits, including profit-sharing, were outstanding; (4) he was told during his interviews that the president of the company wanted to get more young, capable men into top management.

Norman started out with his typical positive approach, but after about three months he slowly became disenchanted and decided he may have made a serious mistake. These were his reasons:

1. He had yet to meet anyone in an important management position who was under thirty years of age—most were over fifty.

2. The company was far more conservative than he had anticipated.

3. Everyone was very patient with him, but they made no bones about the fact that they considered him to be very young.

4. The work climate was somewhat structured and routine, and no one seemed responsive to his ideas.

5. One old-timer told him that he would get a pretty good chance of moving up in about ten years when a lot of the upper management people would be forced to retire.

After talking it over at length with his wife, Norman felt he had but two choices: (1) he could look around and find another company that was more youth oriented, or (2) he could stay with the company on a very determined basis, and through smart human relations, high personal performance, and well-timed aggressive action, make his move to the top despite the obvious handicaps.

Were the handicaps Norman felt real or did they exist only in his imagination? What do you think he should have done? (For suggested answer, see page 205.)

CHAPTER

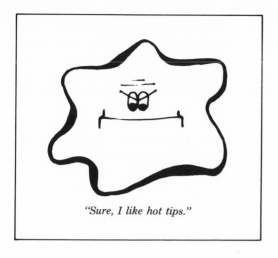

"Sure, I like hot tips."

Thirteen Tips on Succeeding in a New Job or Assignment

Undoubtedly you want to be successful on a new job or assignment. First, you want to prove to your family, friends, and management that you are capable. Second, you want to prove it to yourself. There is a great deal at stake.

This chapter is devoted to thirteen tips that can be of great help to you in reaching this goal. If you take these tips seriously, you will avoid many of the mistakes others make.

TIP 1: Take a Calendar Notebook to Work with You.

An abundance of important information, rules, regulations, and procedures will be thrown at you in the beginning. The first days are days of adjustment and excitement, so don't trust your mind to remember everything. Rather, buy yourself an inexpensive calendar notebook and use it to record some of the tricky instructions and hard-to-remember information you receive from your supervisor or fellow workers. Jot this data down in your notebook, and don't be afraid to do this while the person giving it to you is talking or watching. The notebook itself (if not overused) will create a good impression because it will indicate you are an organized person and are methodical in your approach to learning.

Once you start using a notebook in this manner, you will discover other advantages. It can be used to review certain facts and procedures in the evening to help you prepare yourself for the following day. It can be used for recording appointments, ideas, names, and so on. Perhaps you will eventually form the "notebook habit" as many other successful people have done. It is a habit that will pay big dividends.

TIP 2: Safeguard Your Means of Transportation.

The company you work for will consider it your responsibility to be at work on time, so one of the most injurious things that can happen to you is to report late during your first few weeks—or anytime, for that matter. Whether you have a good excuse or not, reporting late will not enhance your reputation.

If you depend on public transportation, be sure to check the schedule carefully and give yourself plenty of time to make connections. It is much better to be thirty minutes early than three minutes late. If you have your own automobile, be sure you keep it in good mechanical order. Check the tires frequently. Be sure you have sufficient gas. Do some preventive maintenance to protect yourself. Also, allow yourself extra driving time. If you depend on someone else for transportation, be sure he is a dependable person who feels the same way you do about getting to work on time. If you feel he is not dependable, make other arrangements. It is your responsibility to get to work on time. *Management will not be interested in your excuses.*

TIP 3: Conserve Your Energy at the Beginning.

The strain and tension of the first few days and weeks on your new job or assignment will take more energy out of your system than you expect. You will frequently feel drained at the end of the day. As an illustration of this, it is quite common for a new employee to catch a cold and miss a day or two of work during his first weeks of employment. To avoid such a possibility, conserve your energy until you make the adjustment by avoiding a heavy social schedule, eliminating long weekend trips, and refusing to keep excessively late hours. You need to be especially alert during your first few weeks of employment. One way you can prepare for this is by getting plenty of sleep.

TIP 4: Ask Questions, but Learn to Ask the Right Ones.

If you don't understand something, ask questions until you do. This may be necessary because those responsible for your training do not always take enough time to explain things fully. They forget that they often talk too fast and that it is sometimes impossible for you to get the full message the first time around. In such a situation, it is better to ask for a replay so that you will not make the same mistake over and over again. Fear of being considered stupid is the reason most people give for not asking more questions. This is understandable, but it is better to ask questions than to suffer the serious results of continued mistakes.

It is important, of course, to ask the right questions. You should not ask a question when the answer is obvious or when you could find the answer yourself.

There is also a right and wrong time to ask a question. For example, one should not interrupt a person who is concentrating on getting a job done or is communicating with others in order to ask a question that could wait for a more appropriate time.

TIP 5: Use Good Judgment in Working Extra Hours and Taking Your Breaks.

Some new employees, in a futile attempt to secure their job by attracting management's attention, start out by working more than the normal number of hours. They arrive first in the morning and make a point of leaving last at the end of the day. They often skip their breaks. This attitude, if sincere, is to be admired. However, overzealousness can get you into trouble on two counts. First, there are usually regulations governing hours to be worked. On certain jobs, unauthorized overtime work and failure to take breaks can involve you and your employer in labor difficulties. It is important, therefore, to always abide by the instructions given to you by management. Second, your fellow employees may misinterpret your motives and make life more difficult for you and your supervisor. Working extra hours and eliminating breaks when an important deadline must be met and when you are asked to do it by your supervisor is one thing; working extra hours with the sole purpose of impressing others is quite another.

As a rule, it is better to make full use of the time you spend on the job than to try to impress others with your willingness to work extra hours.

TIP 6: Don't Flaunt Your Education and Intelligence.

If you have attended college, chances are good that you will have more formal education than some of the people you will work with on your new job. But since these people may have far more on-the-job experience and practical know-how than you do, it might be smart on your part to let them discover your educational background gradually. You are entitled to be proud of your educational achievements, but you will probably get off to a better start if you don't broadcast it. A good point to remember in this respect is that the job you are assigned may be more difficult than you expect, and if you have tried to impress people with your education or intelligence, they may not offer to give you any help.

Also, you no doubt have learned one way to do things in school or from some previous experience, and you will probably find that things are done differently on your new job. Perhaps your way of doing things is better, but until you are *sure*, be safe and do it the way they do. It will be to your advantage to play a little dumb to begin with. Give the experienced person the satisfaction of explaining how to do things *his* way. This will also give you a chance to build good relationships with your fellow workers. You will have plenty of time later to use your intelligence and apply your education.

TIP 7: Make Friends, but Don't Make Close Friends Too Soon.

There are many little human relations traps you can easily fall into during your first days on a new job. One of these is building one or two very strong friendships at the expense of all others. For example, suppose you discover that one of the girls in your department is extremely friendly the first day. Such friendliness is more than welcome the first few hours in a strange setting. There is a danger, however. What if you spend all your time with her and neglect being friendly to your other fellow workers? What if this friendly person is not respected by the others? What if she has earned a poor reputation in the department and has only selfish reasons for her friendliness towards you? Sometimes people who have failed to earn respect from others at work and have therefore been rejected by them try desperately to win the friendship of the new employee. Remember that it is only natural that the employees (including management) will quickly identify you with any employee or employees you spend excessive time with.

If one employee clings to you as you start your new job, you obviously have a difficult situation to handle. Of course, you should not be rude to this person. You will do well, however, to back away and be somewhat reserved toward this individual for the first few weeks and concentrate on building relationships with *all* people rather than just one.

TIP 8: Look Energetic, but Don't Be an Eager Beaver.

Some young people start their careers with a great burst of energy and enthusiasm that cannot possibly be sustained. These people frequently create a favorable impression to begin with, but later on they are reclassified by both management and their fellow workers. It is easy to be overeager at the beginning. You are new to your job, so you have a fresh and dynamic approach. You have a great deal of nervous energy to release. You are interested, and your interest motivates you to achieve. This desire to succeed, however, might cause you to reach too far too fast. The best way to make progress inside an organization is to make *steady* progress. If you set an unusually fast pace you will have a hard time keeping it up. Furthermore, if you concentrate too hard on getting the job done, you might neglect the people with whom you are working. You will have plenty of time to demonstrate high personal productivity later, but if you move too fast at the start, you may make some serious human relations mistakes that can hurt you in the future.

TIP 9: Different Organizations Have Different Personal Appearance and Grooming Standards.

A few organizations, primarily those engaged in manufacturing, have no personal appearance or grooming standards. They are interested only in your work performance and your human relations ability. What you look like doesn't matter, because only your fellow workers see you. Other companies, especially those that serve customers and therefore must be interested in their public image, are forced to set minimum standards that usually cause no real problem because they are easy to live up to. Still other companies, like fashion-oriented department stores, have rather high personal and grooming standards that may be difficult for a few people to accept. When you join an organization you should carefully assess the situation and decide what is best for you and your future. You are entitled to be yourself, and you have a right to protect your individuality. In making this decision, however, you should weigh all factors and take into consideration that most people, including management, feel that a little conformity won't hurt you.

TIP 10: Read Your Employee Handbook and Other Materials Carefully.

Many organizations spend a great amount of money developing employee handbooks and other materials for new employees. These pamphlets usually contain vital information. Yet, many new employees accept this material, take it home, and never read it. Don't be casual in your use of company literature. Where else can you learn company policies that can keep you out of trouble? Where else can you discover important data that will prevent you from asking unnecessary questions? Take home all of the booklets you receive and devote some time to them. Understanding your company better will help you start on the right foot.

TIP 11: Be Yourself, but Be Your Best Self.

As you go about making your best effort to create a good first impression, it is important that you be natural. You must accept and be satisfied with yourself as you are and not try to copy others. Phony mannerisms will defeat your purpose. You can admire another person, but you cannot *be* that person; you can envy another personality, but you cannot *be* that personality; you can aspire to a reputation for good grooming that another person enjoys, but that does not mean that you should dress *like* that person. If you attempt to copy others, you take the chance of destroying the better facets of your own personality. Just be yourself.

Of course you will wish to be your *best* self, and some of the tips in this chapter and others are designed to help you in this respect.

TIP 12: Listen with Your Eyes As Well As Your Ears.

As far as the person talking to you is concerned, you listen more with your eyes than your ears. Sure, you receive the auditory impressions through your ears; but you give the person speaking your attention with your eyes. Some people feel it is discourteous to let your eyes wander when they are talking to you. You will understand this if you have ever seen someone look at his watch, stare at the floor, or look out a window while you are talking to him. It may seem like a very small point, but you will make better impressions on people if you form the habit of listening with your eyes as well as your ears.

TIP 13: Send Out Some Positive Signals.

One final tip on making good first impressions: A friendly person—one who creates a good first impression—is one who uses certain positive signals when he meets others. He takes the initiative. He makes the first effort. For example, a person with a ready smile is easily interpreted as a friendly person. The smile seems to break any psychological barriers that might exist in a meeting of strangers. You immediately feel accepted by this person. The smile, then, is a friendly signal.

There are many other signals one can use to create a good first impression. "Hello," "Good morning," and "Thank you" are examples of friendly verbal signals. Such easy signals of friendship should be transmitted at every opportunity to acknowledge the presence of others and to recognize any courtesies they have extended to you.

There are also many effective nonverbal signals in addition to the smile. The handshake, a positive gesture with the hand or head, the opening of a door, a friendly facial expression—all these, and many others, are signals you send that make it easier for people to meet and know you. When you send out such signals naturally and in good taste, others do not feel awkward about approaching you. You have made it easy for them, and they like you for it.

People who develop confidence in sending out such signals of friendship make excellent first impressions. They quickly increase their sphere of influence and build many lasting working and personal relationships. Have confidence in yourself and your ability to send such signals. Take the initiative. Send out your own brand of signals in your own style, and be an easier person to meet. You will be pleased with the results.

It is sometimes said that good human relations is little more than good common sense. This statement, of course, has considerable truth in it. The tips presented in this chapter are in themselves common sense. There is no psychological magic here. Simple ideas have been presented in a straightforward manner, yet they can make a difference when actually put into practice. The new worker who reads over this list occasionally during his first few weeks on a job will discover that it can help him make a graceful transition.

PROBLEM

The Eager Beaver

Ed was a fast-moving young man. When he was in college, he was always involved in a wide variety of campus activities. He appeared to have an overabundance of energy, and whenever he was in a group he was rather loud and aggressive. Most of his friends considered him extremely competitive. Ed admitted to himself that he was a poor loser.

Upon graduation from college, Ed received an excellent opportunity with a large but somewhat conservative company. He was assigned to the marketing department. He was eager to get started. He wanted to prove himself quickly, and he started out like a ball of fire. He expressed himself freely in staff meetings, he quickly challenged many traditional ideas, and he engaged those in management positions in frequent conversations. In fact, just a few weeks after he started, the word had gotten around management circles that he was a real eager beaver and was destined for great things inside the company.

What degree of success would you predict for Ed? What are the advantages and the dangers of his approach? (For suggested answer, see page 206.)

"Hank's O.K. . . . he just needs motivation."

The First Weeks Are Critical

"Shape up or ship out" is a Navy term that has become quite common. As used by college students, it often means "get busy and study before you become a dropout." The expression also has a special meaning when you join an organization and are still on a temporary or probationary status. Here it means "adjust quickly to the requirements of your new job or you might get off on the wrong foot and hurt your future or even get fired."

It is not the purpose of this chapter to make you uneasy or tense about your new job. Rather it is designed to help you fully understand just what probationary status means. Many unsuspecting new employees have discovered the true meaning too late. Don't let this happen to you.

There is nothing new about probationary periods in business and industry. All beginning employees have a probationary period. It is traditional. It gives management a last chance to evaluate a person before granting permanent status. It is, in effect, the final screening device in the selection program of a company. You have been interviewed, employed, and given the green light on a temporary basis, but before you are accepted as a permanent employee, management will want to make quite sure they haven't made a mistake.

They have their reasons.

Permanent status is a big thing. It isn't something most companies hand out easily. With permanent status come many things not usually given to temporary employees—vacation benefits, seniority privileges, and profit-sharing, to mention only a few. In some organizations it takes years to achieve permanent status.

For example, you may qualify for a civil service position with the United States government by passing certain oral and written tests. You would then be placed on an eligibility list. If you are at the top of the list and qualify for a position that is open, you may receive a job. Does this mean that you have permanent status? Far from it! In fact, you may be on a temporary status for years before you receive a permanent civil service appointment. Why? Because once you achieve permanent status under the Civil Service Act, you receive many additional advantages. You cannot be terminated except under certain circumstances and through specified procedures. You have certain transfer priorities. You have seniority for certain promotions. You have protection against layoffs. Permanent status with civil service is something to work for over a period of years. It is not achieved easily.

Although most business and industrial organizations do not have such complicated procedures, the same principle applies. Permanent status does not come automatically.

This is also true for most crafts. A young man starts out as an apprentice and works slowly to become a journeyman. He must perform successfully on the job and in the classroom for two to four years before he can become a journeyman. He does not have permanent status until he reaches this goal. Once he receives his certificate, however, he is a recognized journeyman under state law and is given certain privileges and opportunities.

Probationary periods, of course, differ from organization to organization. In some companies it is only a week or possibly thirty days. If you survive, you are considered permanent. Other organizations have probationary periods of two, three, or six months. In some companies it takes a full year to achieve permanent status.

Some organizations are very formal about their probationary periods; others are very informal. If your company has clearly spelled out your probationary period, you know where you stand. If it has not, it would be a smart move on your part to inquire. Don't be fooled about the probationary period just because no one has specifically talked to you about it. Find out for sure. In a month or two it may be too late.

Permanent status does not mean one-hundred-percent job security, but in most cases it is a big step in that direction. Permanent status means a great deal in organizations that have what is called a "promotion from within" philosophy. Many companies make a real effort to employ only those people who are promotable to higher positions. They want to promote from within their own organization. Except in unusual cases, they refrain from employing outsiders for anything except starting or entry jobs. Naturally, a company with this practice would hesitate to give permanent status to someone who could not grow with the company over a period of years.

The information presented above has been designed to show you why you should take your probationary status seriously. Chances are good that it means more than you think it does.

There are two conditions of your probationary status that you should consider in advance.

First, your time may be limited. You may have only a short while to demonstrate your capabilities. Once the time is up, the company must decide whether to keep you or not. So make the most of your time. Don't let it slip by without making your very best effort.

Second, you must change a few habits. Look at it this way: You have just spent twelve to sixteen years in school, or you have resigned a position with a company with different practices and procedures, or you have been out of the labor market for some time and are unaccustomed to the discipline of work. You have formed many habits from your previous experiences or routines. Some of these habits are deeply set. Now, within a few days, *you are expected to change your habits*. The rules may be different. The requirements are different. The procedures are not the same. You must either shape up or ship out.

Can you change your habits? And can you change them in time? Here are a few examples of new employees who failed.

1. Sam received a substantial raise when he moved from one banking organization to another. With ten years of experience in methods and procedures behind him, he had a lot to offer the new company. Sam ran into trouble, however, because he could not adjust. Instead of accepting the new policies and procedures, he constantly compared them with his old company's and tried to change some of them. His constant reference to how things were done at his old company did not set well. Sam was terminated in less than a year.

2. Sue was very popular in school. She had many friends and seldom missed a social event of any kind. The same was true on her first job. Everybody stopped to talk with her, and time went so fast on her breaks that she was often late returning to her desk. Sue didn't realize that excessive socializing was not acceptable in business. She had to lose her first job to discover it.

3. When Gil finished college, he decided he wanted to live a little. He bought a new car, shared a fancy apartment with a high-living friend, and started a promising career with a large company. Gil didn't exactly keep regular hours. Soon this began to have an effect on him and his work. Gil kept his job for just three months before he was released.

Habits that have taken years to form are not easily changed. Poor habits must often be replaced with good habits during an adjustment period. Or, habits that were acceptable in one situation must be replaced with habits that are acceptable in another situation. It often takes real effort, but it can be done.

The truth is that business and industrial organizations expect you to make a quick and satisfactory adjustment to *their* way of doing things. They will try to make things as easy as possible for you, and they will give you all the help that time permits. Beyond that, you are on your own. So make the most of your time.

Your first few weeks and months are also critical for another reason. Most young people accept their first job with an organization on an exploratory basis; in other words, they don't make a firm commitment to themselves to stay with the company until they have had a good chance to respond to the work environment, the work itself, management attitudes, and many other factors. This is a natural attitude, and it is expected and understood by most personnel people. Experience has taught them to anticipate serious misgivings on the part of new employees. Many questions emerge: "Do I really belong here?" "Is this what I really want?" "Did I look far enough before accepting this opportunity?"

If the misgivings are permanent, the employee should seek work somewhere else where he feels happier and more secure. Usually, however, the uncertainty that many new employees experience during their first few weeks or months is just a symptom of a transition period. Some employees become temporarily discouraged because of the unexpected discipline their new job demands; others become frustrated over problems they did not anticipate and were not trained to cope with; still others become disappointed with the routine of the work or the treatment they receive from their supervisor. Most employees make the necessary adjustments easily and live through them without any great trauma. Others have more trouble. Take Hank for example.

Hank was a very impatient, verbal, aggressive, and energetic guy who had to be around people to be happy. It seemed quite natural when he accepted a job with a big retailer where people would appreciate his personality and give him responsibility in a hurry. He started out on the training program they outlined for him with great enthusiasm. Things went very well for a few weeks. Gradually, however, Hank had to face up to the odd working hours that are traditional in the retail business, the great amount of detailed paper work that he didn't anticipate, and a heavy load of problems that required immediate decisions. It all got to Hank after about two months, and he was all set to turn in his resignation. Then his supervisor sensed his dilemma and guided him through the awkward period. Three years later Hank was happy and successful and was certain that he had found the right career and the right company. Of course he also realized that he was lucky to have had a perceptive supervisor.

The following suggestions will be helpful should you become disenchanted with your new job.

1. *Anticipate a few bad days or even weeks.* This may not happen, but it's natural for most employees to have some misgivings about their first job choice. If it happens, realize that it is a normal pattern and that chances are good you will live through it without any serious problems at all.

2. *Give yourself plenty of time.* You will need to give yourself ample time to fully explore and adjust to the opportunity you have accepted, so don't panic the first time something goes wrong. Some experts feel that you should give yourself a full year on a job so that an early negative reaction does not cause a premature resignation. Just remember that most new employees live through touchy periods, and give yourself all the time you need to make a complete personal adjustment and see the overall picture instead of just the immediate problems.

3. *Try to keep a negative attitude from showing.* If you are not careful, you will let your transition problems give you a negative attitude that will be hard to hide, especially from management. If you let a negative attitude become apparent, you might injure relationships that will be difficult to repair later on. There is one other point you should remember. Although it might be wise to talk your adjustment problem over with your supervisor, it is usually best not to discuss it with your fellow employees. They may be unhappy themselves and thus reinforce your negative attitude. They

could indirectly cause you to make a decision you might regret later.

Of course it is possible that your transition to your new job may be smooth and graceful; you may achieve permanent status with little trouble, and the problems brought forth in this chapter may not apply to you. Great! But knowing what *might* happen ahead of time can keep you from making some serious mistakes, and that's what this book is all about.

PROBLEM

11

Tom's Unexpected Termination

Tom was a better-than-average student. Things came easy for him, and he had a casual and relaxed manner. Because Tom was an only child, his parents were in a position to do a great many things for him. It was not necessary for him to work during his school years. He had his own car and a healthy allowance.

Tom had intended to finish college, but in his sophomore year his father became ill and it was necessary for him to quit college and go to work. With the help of an uncle, Tom found employment with a large company in his hometown. It was a fast moving, progressive company with an outstanding reputation for good personnel practices. He was told that he was hired because of his apparent potential for becoming a supervisor.

Tom approached his new job with the attitude that he would give the company about three months to offer him a challenge and an opportunity to advance. In the meantime, he did what he was supposed to do. He put in a good eight-hour day every day. He was friendly. He caused no trouble and made no complaints. It naturally came as a shock when, at the end of sixty days, Tom was called into the personnel office and released. He became very upset and demanded that the personnel director give him a full explanation.

The personnel manager replied in this manner: "As specified in our employee manual, we have a firm sixty-day probation period, which gives us a chance to evaluate the new employee on the job. We feel this is not the right company for you, because you failed to come up with that extra effort that we normally receive from a new employee who is being prepared for a management position. We have all of the average employees we need. All of this was discussed in a management meeting this morning, and the decision was made. I am sorry you are disappointed in us. Perhaps you will find another company that you will like better."

Was the company justified in terminating Tom? Why? (For suggested answer, see page 207.)

CHAPTER

12

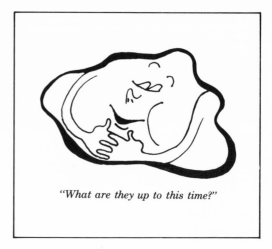

"What are they up to this time?"

How to Handle Teasing and Testing

Getting started in a new job or assignment where the setting is strange and the employees are strangers is bound to give you a few psychological challenges. It is not my purpose to magnify these. Rather, I wish to help you better understand *why* such problems sometimes develop. Even more important, how can you handle them?

Of course management, especially the personnel and training departments, will give you every possible kind of assistance during your first few days and weeks at work. That is their job. But no matter how much they do, chances are that not everyone in the organization will give you an easy time.

You may be assigned to a department as a replacement

for someone the others hated to lose. They will need time to get used to you. You may not have the experience of the person you replace, and as a result others may have to work harder for a few days to get you started. It is even possible that someone in your new department wanted another person to have your job, and there may be some resentment toward you because of this.

It is never easy to be the newest member of a group. You cannot expect to go from being an outsider to an insider without a few adjustments. In the first place, you and your personality were *forced* upon the group; they were not asked whether they wanted you or not. You have, to be very blunt, been imposed upon them. Because they were there first, and because they probably have strong relationships among themselves, they may feel that you should earn your way into their confidence. It may not seem fair, but it is only natural for them to look at your arrival in this way.

Did you ever go through an initiation into a club? If so, you will understand that teasing or testing the new member is often traditional. To a limited extent, the same can be true when a new employee joins a department or division in a business organization. There is nothing planned or formal about it, of course, but you should be prepared for a little good-natured teasing or testing. Let us look at the psychological reasons behind these two phenomena.

The teasing of the new employee is often nothing more than a graceful way of helping the person become a full-fledged member of the group. It is a form of the initiation ritual that will help you feel you belong. Sometimes it is a group effort in which everyone is in on the joke; more often it is an individual matter.

Teasing, for the most part, is harmless.

The shop foreman who has never had the advantage of a college education, but has learned a great deal from practical experience, might enjoy teasing a recent graduate of an engineering school. If the graduate engineer goes along with the teasing, a sound relationship between the two will develop. If, however, he permits it to get under his skin, the relationship could become strained.

The shop foreman's motive might be nothing more than

a desire to help the new engineer build good relationships with the rest of the gang. There may be nothing resentful or personal about it.

A small group of female employees who work closely together in a branch bank, lawyers' office, or similar situation can usually be expected to come up with a little harmless teasing when a new girl joins the staff. She might be given the oldest typewriter with a touch of formal ceremony, the dismal job of keeping the stock room in order, or some humorous instructions on how to approach the only eligible bachelor around.

Usually, this kind of teasing is based upon tradition and human nature. People who like to tease in this manner are generally good-natured. They enjoy people. They mean no harm. In fact, they usually do it to make you feel more comfortable, not less.

If you are on the receiving end of some good, healthy teasing, you have nothing to worry about if you don't take it personally. Just go along with it and you'll come out ahead. It is much better to be teased than to be ignored. If by chance the baiting should go a little too far and you find yourself embarrassed, the very fact that it is embarrassing to you will probably make you some friends. In fact, you will be lucky if there is some mild hazing. It will help you get off to a good start. It will help break down any communication barriers that might exist.

Testing is different. It can have more serious implications. It will take more understanding on your part.

There are two kinds of testing. One is what we may call *organizational testing.* This kind comes from the organization (management, personnel, or your supervisor) and is a deliberate attempt to discover what kind of person you really are and whether or not you can adjust to certain conditions. The other kind comes strictly from individuals. This is *personal testing*—one person trying out another because of personality conflicts or inner prejudices.

Let's look at organizational testing first.

Almost all kinds of organizations—especially the smaller ones—have certain unpleasant tasks that must be done. By tradition these tasks are handed to the newest member. The new salesman in a department store may be given excessive amounts of stock work at the start of his career; the factory worker may be given unpleasant cleanup jobs until another new member joins the department; the clerical employee may be given a nasty filing assignment to start with.

The author joined a large manufacturer and distributor of ice cream upon leaving college, and for the first six weeks he did nothing but stack ice cream in a room where the temperature was below freezing. It was the least desirable assignment in the department and it certainly did not require a college education. After the six-week period, it was possible to look back and see that the assignment was nothing but a planned test. *All* new employees in the department were given this job to start with. It was traditional. It had happened to everyone in the department.

The important thing for the new worker to recognize is that these tests have a purpose. Can the new worker take the assignment without complaining? Can he survive without developing a negative attitude? Or will he show resentment and thereby destroy his chance of gaining the respect of the other members of the department?

The old phrase "starting at the bottom of the ladder" sometimes means exactly that. Many top management people started at the bottom, and they feel that this is the best way for you to start. If you can't take it to begin with, you may not be able to assume heavy responsibility later. It is the price you pay for being a beginner. Management sometimes feels that this is the best way for the manager of the future to fully appreciate the kind of work that must be done by the rank-and-file employee. Many a college graduate finds himself doing the most uninviting tasks to start with. If he is human relations smart he will take it in stride, using the time to size up the situation and learn as much about the organization as possible.

During testing periods you are being watched by management and your fellow employees. *The better you react, the sooner the testing will end and the better your relations with others will be.* In other words, although getting the job done is important, your attitude toward it may be more important. If you react in a negative manner, three things can happen:

(1) you may be kept on the assignment longer than you otherwise would have been; (2) you may hurt your chances for a better assignment later on; and (3) you may damage relationships with those people involved in or observing the testing.

If you can take the long-range perspective and condition yourself to do these tasks with an inner smile and an outward grin, you'll do well for yourself. Roll up your sleeves and get the job done quickly. If you finish one job, move on to another. Don't be afraid to get dirty. If you must take a little abuse, don't complain. It is part of the initiation ritual, and you will look back on it someday as those ahead of you look back on it now. It would be foolhardy for the new employee to fight any of the many forms of organizational testing as long as it doesn't seriously damage his individual dignity.

Personal testing is a different matter. It could give you more trouble, especially if you fail to recognize it for what it is. It may come from someone your own age or someone much older or younger. It may come from a fellow worker or it may come from someone in management. There is nothing wrong with your starting out with the attitude that everything is teasing rather than testing, and if it doesn't last long, you have automatically solved the problem. But if it continues over a long period of time you will know it is personal testing and it comes from deep-seated motives. When this happens, you have a real challenge ahead of you. For example, one of your fellow employees may refuse to accept you; he may harass you at every turn; he may not give you a chance to be a normal, productive employee. The needle will be out at every opportunity.

Ray had this kind of an experience when he was assigned to a maintenance crew with a gas and water company. The job was extremely important to him because it had taken him a long time to get it. He also knew that he was on a very strict ninety-day probation period. Because of this, Ray decided that he would go all out to keep his personal productivity high and still build good relationships with the rest of the crew. Everything would have been great if it had not been for Art, who started out the very first day using every technique in the book to slow Ray down and get under his skin. Art constantly came up with comments like: "What are you trying to do Ray, make us all look bad?" "Who are you kissin' up to by working so hard?" "If you slow down a little, kid, we'll get you through probation."

After three weeks of this Ray knew he was face-to-face with a personality conflict loaded with hostility. Rather than take it any longer, he invited Art to have coffee with him after work one day. It was a strained evening, but Art finally relaxed. Much of the hostility evaporated, and the next day he was off Ray's back. Ray never discovered the real cause of the conflict. The crew seemed happier, and productivity was better.

Although chances are good that it will never happen to you personally, occasionally an employee will be on the receiving end of some nonorganizational, or personal, testing from a supervisor. This is what happened to both Rachel and Jess.

Rachel was happy when she graduated near the top of her class in nursing school. She was even happier when she won her first job as a vocational nurse in a large home for elderly people. But Rachel, a very sincere and conscientious black, quickly discovered that she was on the receiving end of some rather vicious testing from her supervisor.

She was not surprised when she received a lot of ugly jobs her first few days. She knew it was traditional, so she pleasantly went about giving baths to some of the most difficult patients. She had many disagreeable duties, all of which were assigned to her by the supervisor, a registered nurse who had been at the home for many years. Rachel didn't complain, because she didn't want any special favors because she was black. She took everything that came her way, because she wanted to prove to herself that she could take it. But slowly she began to sense there was something more than just routine testing involved. Her supervisor seemed to dish out the ugly assignments with a strange, subtle bitterness. Not only that, but even after two additional vocational nurses had joined the staff, Rachel was still doing all of the really dirty jobs.

Although she was fearful of racial prejudice from the beginning, she tried to play it cool and hope for a change. She said nothing. But soon her fellow workers, most of whom were her age and also vocational nurses, got the message.

When they did a confrontation took place that finally reached the desk of the owner. The pressure on Rachel was quickly removed, and no one was sorry a week later when the registered nurse responsible resigned.

It is sometimes impossible to know the deep seated motive behind some of the serious testing that takes place. Often the people responsible do not know themselves. Racial prejudice is only one of many causes, as the case involving Jess will illustrate.

Jess was really turned on over his new construction job. At last he would be able to put his apprenticeship training to work and make some good money. He anticipated all of the teasing he got from the old-timers at the beginning, and he took it in stride without any big scenes. But the attitude of his foreman was something else. No matter how hard he tried, Jess got the needle from him at every turn; no matter how much work Jess turned out, the foreman was on his back. Jess took it for about a week, and then, in desperation, he asked the advice of one of the older crew members. Here is what the older man said: "Look, Buddy, our beloved supervisor is an uptight conservative. Your long hair, your flashy sports car, and especially your free and easy life style all get to him. Frankly, I think he has had some trouble with his own sons and you remind him of them. At any rate, he's all wrong. What you do to get him off your back, though, is your own problem. Good luck."

Jess gave it some serious thought and decided that he would face the foreman and see what happened. It was a tough decision to make because he didn't want to lose his job. He waited until they could be alone, and then he put all of the cards on the table. He said: "You've been on my back, and you know it! I think you should either tell me why or start treating me the way you treat the others." There were some tense and awkward moments, but when it was all over the foreman managed a small smile, and from then on things were noticeably better for Jess.

The above examples represent only a few of the many different cases that could be presented. Sometimes supervisors are responsible; sometimes they are not. The question is, of course, what can you do if you come up against a serious testing situation.

Here are a few pointers that may help you.

Accept the situation willingly until you have time to analyze it carefully. Take it as part of the test period and conduct yourself in such a manner as to not aggravate it. It may pass by itself, or someone else (without your knowledge) may come to your rescue. If time does not take care of it and you come to the point where you sincerely feel that you are being pushed too far, approach the person who is doing the needling with a "let's lay all the cards on the table" attitude. In your own words, without hostility, say something like this: "If I have done anything to upset you, please tell me. Otherwise I feel it is time we started to respect each other."

This will not be easy for you to do. But in cases of extreme testing it is necessary for the new worker to make the tester account for his actions. There is no other answer.

Unfortunately, some individuals will push you around indefinitely if you permit it. And if you permit it, they will never respect you. Chances are that this will not happen to you, but if it does, you must stand up to the situation and solve it yourself. It is important to you and to the company that you do so.

Of course you should go about it in the right way. Try not to act as though you have a chip on your shoulder. Do not make accusations. Try not to say anything personal about the person you are standing up to. Your goal is to open up the relationship, to find a foundation upon which you can build for the future. You wish to demolish the psychological barrier, not find out who is responsible for it. You must make it easy for the other person to save face. Once the relationship is reestablished, you must follow through and do your share of rebuilding.

You will be better off if you do not go to the personnel department in such situations. You will be respected for taking care of the problem yourself. If, however, you have made every effort to clear it up over a reasonable length of time and you have had no success, you should go to your supervisor and discuss it honestly and freely. Situations of this kind should not be permitted to continue to the point where departmental morale and productivity are impaired.

Do not anticipate such situations. They are very rare. Such a problem may never come your way. For the most part, teasing and testing will be good-natured—even enjoyable—if you take the right attitude toward them.

PROBLEM

12

The Difficult Fellow Employee

Jane graduated from a state college as a home economics major. She was ambitious, talented, and attractive. In practically no time she had a good position with a large utility concern as a demonstrator. After a special training program lasting six weeks, she started putting on demonstration dinners for small groups to show the advantages of the company appliances.

Jane received many compliments on her work from her supervisor and potential customers. She seemed to be able to satisfy everyone but Mrs. Robertson, also a demonstrator, who was a long-time employee of the company. Mrs. Robertson was very critical of Jane. At every turn Jane was the recipient of unkind and seemingly uncalled-for remarks. She began to feel like a piece of granite that Mrs. Robertson was always chiseling on. The older woman even criticized her in the presence of others. Gradually, this began to get on Jane's nerves.

She decided to do something about it. By checking around, she discovered that two girls had resigned because of this woman. This made her feel that there was nothing personal about the trouble she was having. She then discovered that Mrs. Robertson did not approve of many of the new techniques that were being taught in colleges. With this in mind, she waited for the right opportunity to meet Mrs. Robertson alone, and this is what she said;

"Mrs. Robertson, I have been here for two months and I seem to be getting along with everyone but you. I like my job. I want to keep it. If I have done something to offend you, please tell me and I'll certainly make a change. I want very much to win your respect, and even your friendship, but I do not intend to put up with your unfair behavior toward me any longer."

Did Jane do the right thing? Was she too forceful in her approach? What would you have done in her place? (For suggested answer, see page 208.)

"I'm proud of my absentee record."

The High Price
of Absenteeism

"Sorry I didn't show up for work yesterday, Rich. I had a little too much to drink at Harry's party so I decided to stay in the sack and sleep it off."

"Hope things weren't too hard on you last Friday, Alice. I had a case of the blahs, so I stayed home and got a few personal things taken care of."

"Knock it off, Roger, what is sick leave for if you can't steal a day for a special event now and then, or just stay home and take it easy? If you handle it right, the personnel department won't know the difference anyway."

"Did you hear that sick crack from my supervisor, Marge? She sure gets uptight when I'm a little late now and then. You'd think that I'd committed a major crime."

"Don't breathe a word to the boss, Ernie, but I'm going to make this a three-day weekend so I can go on a hunting trip. See you Tuesday."

"I've got to sneak out and take care of something personal, Art. Cover for me while I'm gone, will you?"

You'll hear variations of the above comments inside most organizations today. Absenteeism is a phenomenon that management people live with on a daily basis. So is the problem of lateness and employees leaving their work stations without authorization. Most personnel officers agree that fewer and fewer people are taking pride in their attendance or on-time records. Why?

Those close to the scene have come up with many answers. Here are three that are frequently cited: (1) young people do not commit themselves to a career or company quickly these days, so that during the exploratory stage they do not feel as much pressure to live up to the rules; (2) schools and colleges provide such a relaxing climate these days that the adjustment to the business discipline is more difficult than it was in the past; (3) many people no longer feel they have a moral obligation to live up to absentee standards or rules imposed upon them by organizations.

What is the basic policy that most business and government organizations have toward absenteeism and reporting to work late? What is acceptable and what is not? What is the attitude of management toward the problem, and what action do they take with those who consistently violate their policies?

Most professional personnel managers in business and government will endorse and try to get their employees to live within the framework and spirit of the following policy:

Employees should not come to work when one of the following conditions exist: (1) when it might endanger their own health or that of their co-workers; (2) when the employee is in a psychological or emotional state that could hurt on-the-job productivity and possibly create an unsafe condition; (3) when a serious personal or family emergency exists. If none of the above conditions exist, the employee should be on the job and, except under unusual circumstances, he should be there on time.

The above policy might sound harsh and autocratic, but organizations have had years of experience with the problem and they feel that unless they take a firm stand they will be misinterpreted by some and taken advantage of by others. Here are their reasons for following such a policy.

In order to make a profit and stay in business most organizations must operate under tight production and service schedules. These schedules are built around employees. An assembly line from which a few workers are absent is no longer an assembly line. When a customer wants to buy something in a retail store and there is nobody available to help him, a sale can be lost. When a customer goes to a restaurant and the waitress must do the work of two because another waitress didn't show up, the customer may never return. Management has learned that when an employee or supervisor doesn't show up for work as scheduled, immediate and costly adjustments are necessary if production is to continue and customers are to be kept happy. Sometimes, but not always, a substitute worker can be found; sometimes, but not always, the other employees can pitch in and fill the gap; but most of the time, the company pays at least a small price in loss of efficiency, loss of sales, or loss of customer faith. In short, the absence of an employee usually costs the company money in one way or another. If the absence is necessary, nobody complains. If however the absence is unnecessary, then management must become concerned and involved.

Chronic lateness by an employee, although not usually as serious or expensive to the company as absenteeism, is still a very irritating problem. A late employee can delay the changing of shifts. An employee who is constantly late can emotionally upset a conscientious supervisor and make him more difficult for others to work with for the rest of the day. Most serious of all is the negative influence the consistently late employee has on the productivity of others. The supervisor who takes a soft approach to such an employee stands the chance of losing the respect of the other, more reliable employees.

But absenteeism, lateness, and unauthorized time away from work are not only management problems. They should also be viewed as problems and challenges to the employee himself, and that is primarily what this chapter is all about. How should *you* look at these problems? How will they influence *your* future?

The employee who fails to build a good record in these areas will almost always pay a high price as far as his career's progress is concerned. Here's why.

1. A poor attendance record will keep you from building good horizontal working relationships with your co-workers, because they will resent having to carry an extra load when you are absent.

2. A poor record will strain the vertical working relationship with your supervisor, because it will make more work for him personally, it will cause his department to be less efficient, and it will put him on the spot with other employees.

3. Excessive absenteeism and lateness will build a credibility gap between you and management. This can seriously hurt your future, because those who cannot be depended upon are seldom promoted. It should also be pointed out that, be it right or wrong, some management people feel that there is a moral aspect to the problem. In short, if an individual accepts employment, he agrees to abide by the rules, assuming they are reasonable. Absence without sufficient cause is, therefore, interpreted by these people as a moral failure.

4. Records that reflect heavy absenteeism and lateness are permanent and can be forwarded upon request to other organizations. The record you are building now could help or hurt you should you decide to move elsewhere.

5. If you have a good record, a request to be absent for purely personal and nonemergency reasons will seem more acceptable.

6. In case of layoffs, cut-backs, and reassignments, those

people with poor records are usually the first to be terminated or reassigned.

Most organizations want to be understanding about these problems. They realize that there are exceptions to the rules, and they are willing to listen and make adjustments. Those who consistently abuse the rules are usually counseled in a sensitive manner and are given adequate warnings. Those who play it straight with their companies usually receive fair and just treatment in return. To illustrate the causes and results of absenteeism and lateness among employees and supervisors, the following six examples are cited.

Dennis was a productive worker. When he was on the job and feeling well, nobody could complain about him. He had plenty of skill, a great sense of humor, and he was always willing to pitch in and help others. His only real problem was drinking. Although his supervisor suspected that Dennis had at least a few drinks every day, about every other week he would really tie one on and call in sick. Twelve months ago Dennis and his supervisor had a series of heart-to-heart talks about it. Nine months ago Dennis and the personnel director discussed the problem on three different occasions. Six months ago Dennis was referred to the company physician for any professional help he would accept. Last week Dennis was reluctantly given his termination notice. His record showed that he had been absent over thirty days during the previous year. The organization Dennis worked for had tried to help, but Dennis had refused to help himself.

When she first came to work, Judy showed great promise. She had all of the skills necessary to become a top-flight employee, and she was great with people. Among some of the staff in personnel she quickly became known as the "too" girl. She was too pretty, too vivacious, and too popular. Judy also received too many invitations to too many parties, and as a result, she was absent too frequently. It became rather obvious to Judy's supervisor that she just didn't have the physical endurance to lead such an active social life and, at the same time, hold down a demanding full-time job. During the first six months of employment she was absent eleven times, each time for one day, and her excuse was always illness.

Judy's supervisor, after repeated counseling, finally asked personnel to transfer her to another department. Personnel made an attempt to do this, but when other supervisors checked on her absentee record, they refused to accept her. After additional counseling with little success, management had no other choice than to give her a termination notice.

Bob was highly ambitious, talented, energetic, and respected by both fellow employees and management. Everybody expected him to move a long way up the executive ladder. He seemed programed for success. But Bob's desire for quick recognition and more money caused him to hurt his reputation inside the company. Here is the story. Bob took a moonlighting job with a musical group that was good enough to receive four or five bookings each week. The job paid good money, but it demanded a great deal of energy. After a few months Bob not only looked beat, but his on-the-job productivity started to drop. Soon he started to call in ill occasionally. Within six months he had seriously hurt his reputation. Fortunately for Bob, he had an understanding supervisor and personnel director, and after some counseling, Bob curtailed his moonlighting and started to build back the fine reputation he once enjoyed. It cost Bob at least one promotion, but he did learn that any outside activity that drains one's energy to the point that frequent absences are necessary eventually spells trouble.

Vicki was an excellent sales girl in a fashion department. She was so good, in fact, that she was being trained as a fashion coordinator or buyer. But Vicki had one bad habit she could not shake. She simply could not organize her day to the point where she could get to work on time. Her time card showed that she was from five to fifteen minutes late two or three times each week. Vicki's supervisor, the personnel director, and the store manager all counseled her. Nobody wanted to lose her, but in the final analysis management had to weigh the influence of her lateness on the morale and productivity of others. When this was done, the decision to release Vicki was reluctantly made. She didn't have any trouble getting another job, but the new job didn't have the potential of the one she had lost and the new management was less tolerant with her problem.

Ralph took a job with a business organization to earn money so he could go to law school. The company had a sick-leave policy that granted ten days per year, nonaccumulative. Ralph decided that as long as he would only be around for a year, he might as well be sick once a month so he could use up his sick leave as he went along. Big companies soon become aware of this sort of thing. After being absent five times in five months, Ralph was confronted with the problem, admitted the truth, and was terminated for a basic violation of the sick leave policy. Ralph didn't realize it at the time, but he paid a high price for his five days off.

A national chain organization was having to cut back its work force because of lower sales. It was decided that they could get by with one instead of two employees in a particular department in one of their stores. One individual would be transferred to a less desirable job in another section. A careful analysis was made to see which of the two women should be moved. Both were highly respected, and they were equal in all but two respects. One lady had three years seniority over the other, so normally she would stay. But her absentee record was much poorer than that of the other lady. Management decided that the lady with the best absentee record deserved to keep the better job. When the woman with seniority was notified and given the reason for the decision, she admitted she had no defense.

The above cases are just a few examples of how employees can hurt their long-range careers by frequent absenteeism or chronic lateness. You will be human relations smart if you avoid making the same mistakes. Here are a few tips that will help you:

1. Stay home under the following conditions: (a) when you are honestly sick and you feel it would hurt your health or that of others if you reported to work; (b) if your emotional or mental condition is such that you know you could not contribute to the productivity of the department and you might endanger the safety of others; (c) if you have a family emergency of a serious nature and you are urgently needed at home.

2. Always notify the company of your decision to stay home

by telephone as soon as possible. Tell them in an honest and straightforward way why you can't make it.

3. If you stay at home for more than a single day because of illness, it is human relations smart to give personnel a progress report on your condition and when you will be able to return.

4. Save your authorized sick-leave time for real emergencies. It is a cushion that might come in handy. If you never use it, you should assume the attitude that you were lucky you didn't have to.

5. Always give yourself a little lead time when getting ready to report to work. Do not put yourself in a position where a small delay will make you late. It is better to be ten minutes early than one minute late. On those rare occasions when you are late, give management the real reason for it.

6. Take your allotted breaks, but do not be absent from your work station longer than the specified time. People who always stretch their coffee breaks are not appreciated by their co-workers or their supervisor. When emergencies do come up and you must forgo or delay a scheduled break, don't nurse a feeling that you have been cheated and that you need an extra long break to make up for it.

7. Do not be absent from your work station for long periods of time unless you work it out in advance with your supervisor. Also, let your co-workers and/or your supervisor know where you will be when you are away. The best way to keep a supervisor from breathing down your neck is to earn your freedom by keeping him adequately informed.

8. When you have special reasons for being absent from work, such as family weddings, funerals, or court appearances, work it out as far in advance as possible with your supervisor and the personnel department.

A good record shows management your interest in your job, the company, and its goals. It shows them that you are a motivated rather than reluctant worker. It shows them that you have a positive attitude about your career.

Build a good absentee record, and you'll build a good reputation with management. Maintain a good on-time record, and you'll get along better with your supervisor. Take pride in being a dependable worker and you'll build much better relationships with your fellow workers. Put it all together and you'll be much happier with yourself and your career.

PROBLEM

13

Gary's Decision

It didn't come as a surprise to Gary's friends when they heard he was in trouble with his company because of absenteeism and chronic lateness. It was the same pattern he had followed on campus—always missing classes and always showing up late. Of course it was a little different on campus, because he could turn on his charm and manipulate teachers. With his immediate supervisor, personnel people, and other company managers, it was a different thing.

Gary was called on the carpet for the third time three months after he started the management training program. Everybody was nice in his approach to the problem, but it was finally made clear that Gary should either start changing his habits or consider another career. The strange thing about it all was that Gary really wanted to be successful. It was a good job. It was a fine company. In addition, Gary wanted to get married soon, and without a good job the prospects were not attractive. Why had he permitted himself to build such a poor record? Here are three reasons: (1) he had underestimated how difficult it would be to change the habits he had developed in school; (2) he couldn't bluff as easily in the world of business; (3) he failed to get the message that by being late or absent he was hurting his relationships with others because it put an extra burden on their shoulders.

At any rate, Gary admitted that it was his own fault that he had started off on the wrong foot. He did have a poor record as far as absenteeism and lateness were concerned. He did have a reputation for being undependable. Now he had a very difficult decision to make. Should he stick with this company, try to change his habits, and work hard to live down the poor record? Or should he resign and start over with a new company?

What would you advise Gary to do? (For suggested answer see page 209.)

CHAPTER

"Me? Make a mistake?"

Three Common Human Relations Mistakes

You will make a few small mistakes in human relations every day that you live. This is to be expected. Interviews with key personnel and management people, however, show that in business operations today there are three common mistakes that are most damaging to one's on-the-job happiness and personal progress. It is the purpose of this chapter to single out and fully explain the implications of these three mistakes:

1. Failure to listen.
2. Underestimating others.
3. Failure to report or admit mistakes to management.

Failure to Listen

Many excellent books and articles have been written about

the art of listening. Some of these have been written by specialists after considerable research. Your public library will help you find worthwhile material on the subject. Our discussion of it will be brief and to the point.

The statement that many people in our society need to *learn how to listen* may at first sound strange to you. How can you train your auditory senses to hear better? What can you do to guarantee that the sounds around you are better transmitted to your brain? Nothing, of course, unless you actually have a hearing problem and need a hearing aid. Your problem is not hearing; the sounds around you are reaching your brain. *Your problem is concentration.*

Hearing is a selective process. You can, with concentration, hear what you want to hear. Your problem, then, is to learn to listen to what is important and push other sounds to the outer edge of your hearing. There are so many sounds around you that you may not be picking up the ones that are vital to your happiness and success.

On the job, hearing is a matter of practical communication. When a supervisor or fellow worker wishes to transmit an idea, a warning, or a change in procedure to you, he must in many cases do this verbally. There may not be time for written communication. He must say or transmit the message to you to the best of his ability. Conditions may not be ideal for him. There may be other sounds he cannot eliminate. The working day may be ending, and you may be tired. His words may mean one thing to him and another to you. Good, clear, accurate communication is never easy.

Let us assume, however, that the person initiating the message does the best job possible. Does this ensure that you will receive the message? Of course not! You are the receiver, and if your mind is focused elsewhere when the message is transmitted, *you may hear the sounds but fail to get the message.*

It is evident that communication is a complicated process. It is not easy to be a good sender or a good receiver. Let's take a closer look at the problem.

Advertising executives and specialists have recognized for years how difficult it is to get the verbal message home. This difficulty is most apparent in television commercials, in which the name of the product is often repeated six times in thirty seconds. If you are really listening, you might feel that such repetition is an insult to your ability to receive. You would be justified in this reaction. But the advertising people do not assume that you are a good listener. They assume that you are a *typical* (that is, poor) listener. Consequently, in order for the product name to make an impression, they pound it home through repetition.

Your supervisor is not an advertising expert, nor does he have the time to pound his message home. He feels he should be able to say it once and you should receive it. He assumes you are a good listener.

You often hear a mother say that she must shout and yell to get the message across to her young son. As sender, she is in a frustrating position. "He just doesn't listen to me anymore," she says. And the son may have the same complaint: "There's no use talking to my mother. She just doesn't listen, so how can she understand me?" Perhaps both mother and son have forgotten how to listen.

This can happen to people with the best of intentions. Sometimes it is very difficult to just sit back and listen. We are often so busy with our own thoughts and desires that we are 90 percent sender and 10 percent receiver. When this happens, the communication system breaks down.

In business and industry, the ability of the employee to listen is often a matter of dollars and cents. A draftsman who doesn't hear an architect tell him to make a certain change in a blueprint can cause the loss of thousands of dollars when a bid is accepted on specifications that are not correct; a salesman who fails to hear a message from a client, and therefore does not comply with an important delivery date, can lose not only the sale but also a valuable customer. Communications problems can also cost money inside factories. For example, the failure of Daniel to receive and retain the right message from his shop foreman cost his company a considerable amount of money a few weeks ago. Here is the story.

Dan, on his way to his regular morning coffee break and somewhat preoccupied with his own thoughts, was stopped by his foreman and told to change the tolerance on a machine part he would be turning out for the rest of the day. After his coffee break, Dan returned to his machine, made an adjustment, and worked hard the rest of the day to complete all of the parts. The following day he was called on the carpet for producing parts that were too small. What had happened? Dan had been told to *increase* the size of the part, but he had *decreased* it. His failure to receive—and retain—the right message was a serious mistake, and it cost his company money in terms of both time and materials.

You can think of many other examples. It can even be said that when safety precautions are the subject of the message, the ability to listen can be a matter of life or death.

Let's look at your ability to listen from the viewpoint of your supervisor who is, after all, the primary sender of important messages to you. Here are four questions you can ask yourself to determine whether you are a good listener:

1. Does your supervisor have to fight to get your attention?
2. Do you find yourself thinking of something else the moment he starts talking?
3. Does he voluntarily repeat the message? Or do you find you must go back and ask him to repeat it?
4. Do you sometimes feel confused over instructions given to you when you start to do the job requested?

If you can say no to these questions, you may be a good listener. If you cannot, you should concentrate on improving. The following tips should help you.

1. Always look at the person who is sending the message; this will help you to concentrate and close out unimportant noises.
2. If your supervisor has trouble sending clear signals, you must make the extra effort to listen more carefully. Although it is primarily his responsibility to be a good sender, it is still to your advantage to receive the message if at all possible.
3. So that you will remember the message once you receive it, jot it down in your notebook. Repeat it in your own mind a few times. Put any change ordered in the message

into practice as soon as possible. When appropriate, repeat the message to your supervisor.

Being a good listener is not easy. It will take a conscientious effort on your part, but one of the finest compliments
you will ever receive will be something like this: "One thing
I really like about him is that if you tell him something once
you know he has got it. You never have to tell him twice."
Being a good listener will pay handsome dividends!

Underestimating Others

The second of the three big mistakes, according to personnel
people, is that of underestimating others, particularly those
in management positions. One of the mistakes you can make
most easily is to underestimate the contribution of another
person to the productivity of your organization. As a non-
supervisor new to the organization, you are not expected to
see the big picture. Your view is somewhat limited by the
role you play in the organization. You have no way of knowing
the multiple responsibilities faced by other people. A management or nonmanagement person may not appear to be doing
very much from your limited perspective; you might wrongly
assume that he is coasting. This could be a big mistake. The
person who looks busiest is not always the most productive.
You are estimating without knowledge of responsibilities and
contributions that only top management can see.

Here is a simple case to emphasize the point.

Helen accepted a job with a major metropolitan department store. After thirty days of training she was temporarily
assigned to the basement operation and put in charge of a
Mrs. Smith, who was the manager of inexpensive women's
apparel.

Helen soon discovered that she was part of a rather hectic
operation. Merchandise moved in and out of the department
quickly. Racks and counters were messy and disorganized.
Mrs. Smith was not an impressive person to Helen. Her desk
was disorderly. She seemed to move in many directions at
the same time. She seemed to spend more time than necessary just talking to the employees.

Helen decided that she had drawn an unfortunate first assignment and wished she could move to the upper floors where there was more prestige and where the managers seemed to be better organized.

It was her good luck, however, to meet a young buyer at lunch one day. From this woman she learned that Mrs. Smith had the most profitable department in the store and an outstanding reputation with all top management people. Mrs. Smith had trained more of the store's executives than any other person. It was then obvious that Helen had received one of the best assignments and had been guilty of underestimating Mrs. Smith.

The new employee in this case learned a big lesson without getting hurt, because she quickly changed her attitude toward Mrs. Smith before the relationship was seriously damaged. She was fortunate.

The danger is great when you fail to build a good relationship with a supervisor or a fellow employee because you underestimate him.

You, as a new employee, are in the poorest position to estimate the power, influence, and contribution that others are making to the organization, *especially when these people are already in management positions.* You will be smart to avoid prejudging others. Different people make different contributions to the growth and profit of an organization. Top management can usually see this, but you may not.

If the temptation is too great and you must at times question the effectiveness of others, keep your impressions to yourself. You can easily trap yourself by being a grandstand quarterback. Underestimating the value of others can cost you a great deal in personal progress.

Failure to Report or Admit Mistakes to Management

The third common human relations mistake is failure to admit or report to management personal goofs, errors in judgment, or violations of company procedures, rules, and regulations.

Everyone makes a minor slip or even an occasional blunder.

Even a good employee is not perfect. Precise and methodical people sometimes make mistakes in calculations. Logical thinkers who pride themselves on the scientific approach to decision making will sometimes make an error in judgment. A conscientious person who is very loyal to his organization will, on occasion, violate a company rule or regulation before he knows it.

These things happen to the best of people, and unless you are a most unusual person they will happen to you. These little mistakes will not damage your career if you admit them openly. They can, however, cause considerable damage if you try to cover them up and in so doing compound the original mistake. To illustrate, let us take the incident of the dented fender.

Ken had started his career with a large banking organization six months before. One of his numerous responsibilities in his first assignment was to deliver important documents to various branch operations in the banking system. To do this, he would check out a company car from the transportation department.

On one such an assignment, Ken put a slight dent in the right rear fender of a company car while backing out of a crowded parking lot. He knew that he should report the damage to the dispatcher, but the dent was so insignificant that he thought it would go unnoticed. Why make a federal case out of a little scratch? Why spoil a clean record with the company over something so unimportant?

Two days later Ken was called into the private office of his department manager. He had an embarrassing twenty minutes. He had to admit that he was responsible for the damage and that he had broken a company rule by not reporting it. The incident was then closed.

The slight damage to the company car was a human error anyone could make. The *big* mistake Ken made was not reporting it. Looking back on the incident, he admitted to himself that the damage to the car was far less than the damage to his relationships with others.

Most little mistakes, and perhaps many big mistakes, are quickly accepted and forgotten when they are openly and quickly reported. But to throw up a smoke screen to cover them up is to ask for trouble in a big way. The second mistake may be far more damaging than the first.

It is human relations smart to openly admit your mistakes. It will strengthen your relations with management in the long run.

PROBLEM

14

The Poor Listener

Fay was a graduate of a metropolitan art institute that had an outstanding reputation. She was twenty-one years old, attractive, talented, and vivacious. The instructors at the institute were so pleased with her work that they went out on a limb to help her get her first job with a large advertising agency.

After a few weeks on the job it became obvious to everyone that Fay had unusual talent; it also became obvious that she was a great talker but a lousy listener. She would bubble over in communicating her own ideas, but the moment someone else started to talk her attention would drift elsewhere. One person interpreted this behavior as a form of discourtesy and tried to stay clear of Fay.

Her job consisted primarily of doing preliminary sketches and renderings of certain assorted products, forms, and symbols that were communicated to her verbally by her supervisor, a talented artist himself. Often he would take only a few minutes to explain what he wanted and then leave Fay to work away for the rest of the day. Although her finished artwork was very exciting, he soon became impatient with her inability to produce work even remotely related to the ideas he gave her verbally. Most of what she turned in had to be thrown away. After giving it some serious thought, Fay's boss came to the conclusion that she got so emotionally charged when discussing various art concepts that she just didn't hear what other people, including himself, said. Finally he called her into his office and told her she would either have to learn to listen or he would have to recommend her release. He said he would give her two weeks to make the change.

Was Fay's boss justified in his impatience and the action he finally took? What suggestions would you make to her

in order to solve the problem and save her job? (For suggested
answer, see page 210.)

"Another rumor on its way."

Beware of the Rumor Mill

Webster's New World Dictionary gives us this definition of the word *rumor*: "General talk not based on definite knowledge; mere gossip; hearsay; an unconfirmed report, story, or statement in general circulation."

Unauthenticated reports, or rumors, seem to originate and circulate within every group of people, especially when members of such a group have common interests and competitive goals. Rumors are common in small communities, social and service groups, schools, churches, and, of course, business organizations. They seem to have found a special home in military establishments.

The birth and circulation of rumors seem to be natural phenomena based on the need of people to share their anxieties with others. Some rumors get started because of faulty communication or unintentional misinterpretation of the original message; others are in the form of malicious gossip designed to hurt another person.

Two popular expressions have become associated with the circulation of rumors. One is *rumor mill.* This familiar expression implies that rumors, like grain being processed in a mill, are turned out regularly in large numbers, altered, and circulated within the confines of a certain group or organization. The mill never stops grinding.

The second popular expression is *grapevine,* which means an unofficial, confidential, person-to-person chain of verbal communication. The grapevine can best be viewed as an underground network that operates within an organization. The rumor mill may get the message started but the grapevine keeps it moving. The grapevine has the reputation of operating without official sanction, and usually the information transmitted has an aura of secrecy.

Both expressions are coined, or slang, phrases. They should not be taken literally, but they should be taken seriously. They are used to tell us that rumors have a way of starting and traveling.

Although the opposite is often implied, not all information that gets into the rumor mill and travels along the grapevine is false. It can be the truth, providing the person who introduces the information has the facts right and they are transmitted without misinterpretation. These conditions, of course, are seldom present; even when the original information is accurate, facts often become distorted as they move along the grapevine.

The important thing to realize is that information tossed about in the rumor mill and passed along the grapevine is *not* reliable.

It may not be based upon the facts. But it may be slanted to serve the purpose or wish of a second, third, or fourth person. It may even be malicious.

For these reasons the rumor mill should be viewed with considerable caution, and information coming through the grapevine should be discounted. You cannot depend on it.

Since rumors occur in all forms of organizations, it is only natural to find them in business and industrial concerns, and it follows that there may be a rumor mill in your organization. If there is, be forewarned.

What is management's position in this matter? This book, of course, cannot speak for your management. However, this can be said: the term *rumor mill* is not new to those in leadership positions and management usually knows when a grapevine exists.

This does not mean that the people responsible for management condone the grapevine, but they know when it is in operation. We know this because they occasionally step in and squelch a false rumor before damage is done to either an individual or the company.

The new worker should realize that keeping all employees fully informed on all company matters of concern to each is a Gargantuan task. The use of conferences, bulletins, company periodicals, and other media never seems to be adequate for all employees. But even if official forms of communication were fully adequate, it is doubtful that rumors would be eliminated. Management knows this. So if you are on the recieving end of rumors in your job and you sense the existence of a rumor mill, this does not mean that management is not concerned. It is!

Those in leadership positions are aware that unfounded rumors can cause unnecessary anxiety among employees and that such anxiety hurts the morale of the organization. They know that efficiency drops when personnel are unsettled by information that is false or half-true. They know that rumors can sometimes be malicious, and that innocent employees can be hurt. They will do what they can to prevent this.

In order to be successful, however, they need the help and support of every employee.

What might you do to help management? And more important, what might you do to help yourself? Here are six suggestions.

1. The first thing is to admit that there *is* such a phenomenon as a rumor mill in your organization. If you are blind to this situation you may introduce and transmit harmful rumors to others without knowing it.

2. All information received through the grapevine, especially if it has implications of intrigue, should be interpreted with skepticism, and you should not permit this information to disturb you personally. If it is true, you will have time to adjust to it after you receive it from official sources. Be patient until you get the facts. Partial information is dangerous. Give management time to give you all the facts. Do not take any action or make decisions until you *know*.

3. Do not be guilty yourself of introducing rumors into the grapevine. You may, by accident, overhear something of a confidential nature and pass it on to someone as the truth, only to discover at a later date that you only heard part of the story. Or you may see something a little unusual and draw an erroneous conclusion, as in the following case.

Rebecca noticed her supervisor, a young married man, taking Florence, a co-worker and older divorcee, home two nights in succession. She decided there was something going on between them and introduced the matter into the local grapevine. As so often happens, the rumor got out of hand. A number of people, including Rebecca, got hurt, because the supervisor was transferred and his replacement was harsh and demanding. What was the truth? Florence had found it necessary to put her car in the garage for two days, and the supervisor had volunteered to take her home so that she would not have to walk the dark streets alone. There was nothing more involved.

4. Refuse to pass on unsubstantiated information you receive secondhand. If you do this, you may break the circuit in the grapevine and perhaps keep others from becoming disturbed unnecessarily.

5. If you must complain about company matters or company people, do so in the proper manner to your immediate supervisor, or blow off steam at home or with a trusted person away from your fellow workers. This will eliminate the possibility of having your personal gripes misinterpreted and introduced into the rumor mill. It will also keep anyone from using your complaints to hurt your relationships with your superiors.

6. Try not to permit a nonpersonal rumor, but one that might involve your future with the company, to upset you personally until you get the facts. If you do, there might be a noticeable drop in your personal productivity that will needlessly hurt your future. Make every effort to ignore the rumor until you receive official information. If you find you cannot do this, consult your supervisor or someone else in management for the facts before you draw unwarranted conclusions. Many employees have injured their future by premature action based upon a false rumor. Don't fall into this trap.

We could fill pages discussing the various kinds of rumors that travel along the grapevine. We could give many examples. It will serve our purpose best, however, to place them all into the following two broad classifications.

Many on-the-job rumors involve people's personal lives and are not related to job situations. Some of these fall into the back-fence category; some are little more than coffee-break gossip. They are important in the world of work *only* when they influence productivity. Although there is a considerable intrigue to such rumors, the new employee would be human relations smart to keep working relationships strictly *working relationships* and stay a safe distance from such rumors.

Rumors of the second kind concern the *organization*. They pertain to things that may or may not happen to tᴖe company itself. Although they influence employees, they are not personal. For example, there have been rumors about layoffs with no foundation in fact, rumors that departments were to be eliminated when in fact they were to be enlarged, rumors of resignations when in fact none were ever contemplated, and rumors of terminations that turned out to be transfers. Organizational rumors have great influence on the productivity of employees and the general progress of the company; and management, by keeping the official channels of communication open, tries to eliminate them. Some continue to exist in most companies, however, and unless the employee develops a way to insulate himself against them, he can become constantly insecure about his job and his future. His personal productivity will go up and down based upon the latest rumor. And all for nothing!

For a moment, let us look closely at one aspect of the problem from a positive point of view. Have you ever heard the phrase *confidence triangle*? It is a simple way of describing how and why a confidential comment can be transmitted with considerable impact to a third party. The diagram below will help explain the idea.

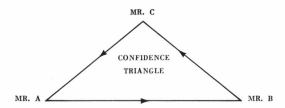

MR. C

CONFIDENCE
TRIANGLE

MR. A   MR. B

We will assume you are Mr. A. You have a strong, healthy relationship with Mr. B. Occasionally you talk things over with him in confidence. One day at lunch you mention that Mr. C has been of great help to you in completing a certain project, and that you have considerable respect for his ability and perception.

You do not realize, when you say this, that Mr. C has a strong relationship with Mr. B and that your comments will be transmitted to him. Of course this will not hurt your relationship with Mr. C. In fact it will improve it, because these favorable comments have been made in confidence, and Mr. B could have repeated them where you might have found them embarrassing.

So far the confidence triangle has worked in a positive manner. *But what if your comments had been negative?*

Instead of improving your relationship with Mr. B, you could have damaged it. The confidence triangle works both ways. The truth is, then, that you can strengthen or weaken relationships with some people *through others*.

Nobody likes to accept advice. Even when advice comes at the right time from the right person in the right way, it is difficult to accept. Yet, sometimes accepting advice is the smart thing to do.

Let us assume that at this very moment the conditions

are ideal and you are willing to accept advice. What might be the best human relations advice you could receive? In all probability it would be this:

If you can't say something good about a person, don't say anything at all.

Like most advice that comes in such simple terms, this precept is far easier to put into print than to put into practice. Yet the degree to which you observe this simple rule on your new job will have considerable influence on your success.

Understanding the nature of rumors, the power of the rumor mill, the scope of the grapevine, and the impact of the confidence triangle should teach you to be *most* careful about what you say to others.

It has been said that many human relations problems one faces are self-created problems. There is truth in this statement.

PROBLEM

15

Sylvia's Dilemma

Sylvia was twenty-four years of age, serious minded, well educated, capable, and very attractive. Although she fully expected to be married in a few years, until the right person came along she wanted some management experience. She had been trained for it in college, so why shouldn't she have it?

Sylvia worked hard for three years. She did an excellent job in human relations. Her personal productivity was never questioned. Mr. Smith, her supervisor, encouraged her to prepare to take over his job. Although he helped her a great deal in this respect, he, of course, made no promises.

About this time, Sylvia spent the evening with Helen, an intimate friend of hers. They had a few drinks and a lot of conversation. At one point Helen told Sylvia that she had heard that a Mr. Young, an employee from another department, was being trained to take Mr. Smith's place as department head. Although she said nothing and did not show it on the outside, Sylvia was very disturbed by the news. It was hard to believe that management could make such a decision so far in advance. She fretted about it constantly and could not keep her mind on her work. As a result, she made more and more mistakes, and certain important reports were turned in late. Over the next six months the excellent relationship she had with her supervisor slowly deteriorated.

Then, just as Helen had said, Mr. Smith was promoted and Mr. Young was made department head in an official announcement from top management. Sylvia was deeply hurt and disappointed.

What mistakes did Sylvia make that might have contributed to her ultimate disappointment? (For suggested answer, see page 211.)

16

"I'll show 'em!"

PFW Can Mean Opportunity

If you go about it in the right way, you can build a rich and rewarding career within the framework of a single organization instead of moving from one company to another. The practice that makes this possibility exciting is called *promotion from within*. We will call it PFW.

What is PFW? How does it work? How might it influence your career? What are the advantages and disadvantages? Do all organizations have such a policy?

There is nothing new about PFW. It has always been the custom to move those who demonstrate they are capable and responsible into higher positions when vacancies occur. If the right people are available, *management wants to promote from within the company's own ranks.* This policy builds loyalty, provides motivation, encourages longevity, and has many other advantages. Many large banking, retail, insurance, transportation, and industrial organizations have strong PFW policies. A few have made it the keystone of their entire philosophy. It should be remembered, however, that even the company that has such a policy must make a few exceptions. Management may find it necessary to bring a few outsiders, such as lawyers, architects, research specialists, and tax experts, into key staff positions.

In order to understand the implications of the PFW idea in the modern corporation, one first needs to understand the great complexity of the organizational structure. Every company has grown to maturity in a different way. Every company has a history all its own. Every company has its own interpretation of PFW.

Because of this, generalizations are very dangerous, and the reader must interpret the following pages in the light of policies and practices of his own comapny. One cannot presume to speak for all of management.

It is important, however, to give the new worker a perspective on his career possibilities. The triangle shown will get us started.

This diagram could represent a business, industrial, or governmental organization. Size is not important. It could be a company with 200,000 employees or with 200. Management—those people who are responsible for the leadership and direction of the company—are of course at the apex of the triangle. Small outfits may have only a handful of management people; large industrial combines may have thousands spread over the world.

Some organizations divide management into four classifications: top management, middle management, junior management, and supervisory positions.

Top management executives with giant concerns are usually the president and vice-presidents; middle management people are usually division heads and branch and plant managers; junior management includes middle management assistants, those whose positions fall just beneath the middle management classification. Next in line come the many supervisors.

Below the management level are many kinds of personnel, depending on the type of organization. In a manufacturing business we find different levels of technical people: engineers, technicians, skilled craftsmen, semiskilled workers, and helpers. In other kinds of organizations there are different patterns and different backgrounds.

Supervisory positions, as illustrated above, can outnumber higher management positions. There is usually a supervisory position for every twelve employees in an organization; in some companies the ratio is lower. The supervisory position is extremely important to the new worker, for in most cases this is the first position leading to upper management.

Now that we have seen the top of the triangle, let us look at the bottom. All organizations employ the majority of new workers at lower-level entry positions. This is where you, the new employee, will no doubt start. Of course in most companies there are different entry levels, depending on experience and education. With rare exceptions, however, all are close to the bottom. The following diagram will illustrate four possible entry levels for those leaving school with little or no experience.

TOP MANAGEMENT

MIDDLE MANAGEMENT

JUNIOR MANAGEMENT

SUPERVISORY POSITIONS

FOUR-YEAR COLLEGE GRADUATES
TWO-YEAR COLLEGE GRADUATES
HIGH SCHOOL GRADUATES
NON-HIGH SCHOOL GRADUATES

Not all companies have four entry levels. Some have only two or three. The important thing is that they are all relatively close together. Regardless of the amount of education, almost everyone starts near the bottom.

The level of the entry position, important as it may be, is not as important as the fact that all employees have an opportunity to *grow*. Each employee, regardless of where he starts, can and should move upward in the organization. No one is stuck forever with his entry position. This is the meaning of PFW.

A natural assumption is that the more education or experience the employee has, the greater his growth potential. Another natural assumption is that the more education or experience a person has, the *faster* he can grow within the company. In other words, the college graduate or the experienced man is expected to move up the ladder farther and faster than the high school graduate on his first job.

Let us assume that four young men join a company at the same time. One has not finished high school; one has a high school education; one has had two years of college; one has a four-year college degree. Where might the company expect these four men to be in thirty years? The diagram below will give you an idea.

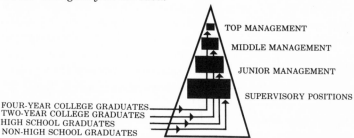

TOP MANAGEMENT

MIDDLE MANAGEMENT

JUNIOR MANAGEMENT

SUPERVISORY POSITIONS

FOUR-YEAR COLLEGE GRADUATES
TWO-YEAR COLLEGE GRADUATES
HIGH SCHOOL GRADUATES
NON-HIGH SCHOOL GRADUATES

The four-year college graduate, providing he was the right person and practiced good human relations, *could* be farthest up the ladder, perhaps in a top management position. The two-year college graduate, providing he was the right person and practiced good human relations, *could* be ahead of the high school graduate and in a junior or middle management position. The high school graduate could have made it to a junior management position; even the non-high school graduate (with perhaps some special help provided by the company) could have made it to a supervisory position.

All can make progress. All can experience growth. The only difference is the distance they go and their rate of progress.

This, of course, is all hypothetical. Does it always happen that way? Not necessarily. *Under the merit system there are no guarantees.*

PFW does not give the college graduate a sure ticket to move ahead faster. He *should* move ahead faster. Management *expects* him to move ahead faster. He is often given special training to help him move ahead faster. But there is no guarantee. He still must earn his way with high productivity and he must still be human relations smart.

Remember that under normal circumstances the high school graduate at the time of employment should be four years younger than the colllege graduate. He will have had four years of training before a college graduate his own age joins the company. These four years are learning years— apprenticeship years. In this four-year period the high school graduate should have made considerable progress with the company. If he takes advantage of his training, he can have his career well under way by the time a college graduate his age joins the company.

This is not to underestimate the value of additional education in building a lifelong career. The more education the better. An organization must protect itself by having the proper blend of four- and two-year college as well as high school graduates. It must look ahead twenty and thirty years. There is room in all organizations for all levels of ability, aptitude, and creative talent.

The difference between educational backgrounds of workers is a human relations problem in itself. You know the story. The college graduate may feel he is not given opportunity fast enough; the noncollege person feels that graduates are given opportunity too fast. Management needs both and recognizes the need to give both growth opportunities. But one thing should be made clear:

The college graduate does not arrive at the top because of the degree itself. If he arrives at all, it is because he had a greater potential and he *used* it.

By the same token, the new worker is not restricted because he does not have a degree. He can still arrive at the top and sometimes does. This may not be as universally true today as it was years ago, but it is still true. Remember there are different ways and different routes, by which a person reaches the top. And what is to keep the ambitious noncollege person from continuing his education at night? He may or may not eventually receive a degree, but his work in that direction will improve his potential.

A college degree is often more important to the person who doesn't have it than it is to the person who does. The danger to the noncollege person is that he permits the degree to become a psychological block. A person doesn't stop growing and learning just because he has less formal education than others. In most organizations opportunities lie in so many different directions that the noncollege employee can find excellent opportunities open to him.

There is also a real danger for the college person. He may expect his college degree to automatically open doors. He may want too much too fast. He may expect too much status from his job at the start. In most instances he must add to his college training the practical experience the noncollege person already has before he can expect to move upward. It takes time to capitalize on a college education.

The many factors involved in building a lifelong career within the framework of a single company cannot all be discussed here.

There is such a thing as being at the right place at the right time with the right preparation to win a promotion.

There is such a thing as having the right level of aspiration—to expect enough, but not too much, from oneself.

There is such a thing as growing with a growing company. If the company is expanding, positions open up more frequently.

There is another approach to the whole matter of career planning.

For example, it is easy to build a case that certain highly aggressive and nonconforming individuals should not attempt to stay inside a strong PFW company. They are simply not geared for long, secure, but frequently slow climb to the top. Rather, they should seek out companies that do not have a firm PFW policy and take the zigzag route to the top by moving from company to company whenever they can improve their position.

In other words, just as there are advantages in working for a strong PFW organization, there are also disadvantages. Here are three primary advantages.

1. Young people who join PFW companies compete *only* with those inside the company for better positions. They do not have to worry about outsiders who might be hired to fill positions they aspire to. Everyone starts near the bottom, and theoretically everyone has a chance to compete, despite differences in education and experience. When someone at the top retires, a chain reaction can open up many positions all the way down the organizational ladder.

2. Organizations with PFW policies are forced to provide good training for their employees so that they are ready to assume more responsibility when opportunities arise. This usually means that more on-the-job time is spent on training of all kinds. It also usually means that such companies will encourage their employees to continue their formal education and will often pay the bills. Because of this, employees are less likely to be ignored or lost in the shuffle.

3. Almost everyone is provided a high degree of job security and a growth pattern that, as far as possible, fits his individual needs. Everyone is encouraged to reach his or her own potential. Fewer people find themselves at a permanent dead end early in their careers. More individual counseling and consideration usually takes place.

Just as there are many advantages, there are also disadvantages. Here are three.

1. Many highly ambitious people who work for PFW companies claim that promotions come too slowly. People are trained too far ahead of time. There is too much waiting. These are usually the same people who claim that the best way to the top is to move from company to company instead of sticking it out with one organization.

2. The human relations role is more critical because both management and nonmanagement people seldom leave the organization and seldom forget anything. In short, a person who makes a serious human relations mistake inside a PFW company must live with it longer, because the people affected will be around to remember.

3. More conformity may be necessary. PFW organizations seem to build a company identity that pulls people together but at the same time leaves less room for individual freedom. For some people this could be a serious disadvantage.

As you look ahead—as you plan your career—take the following factors into consideration. Although they can be important in other organizations, *they are doubly important inside a PFW company.*

- A company interested in it's future must employ young people more on the basis of what they can learn in the future than on what they have learned in the past. It is the capacity to grow that is important.

- The longer you stay with a given company the more opportunities open up for you providing you continue to learn and maintain good human relationships.

- Take the broad learning approach during your early years. Move horizontally into every possible department, whether the move gives you an increase in pay or not. All experience has value as far as preparing you for positions further up the management ladder.

- Discover and study the various lines of progression in your company. Attempt to move up through the channel that best suits your ability.

- Within bounds, do not fear being aggressive. Submit ideas that have been well researched. Communicate upwards.

- When a position becomes vacant, let management know in the right way that you are interested. Do not assume that they know. It doesn't hurt your relationships with others to ask.

· Good relationships with supervisors built early in your
career can pay off later. For example, the first supervisor
you have may be someone who is going somewhere in
your organization. If you demonstrate your ability to him,
he may be able to pull you along with him.

Most executives in business, industrial, and governmental
organizations realize the advantages and responsibilities of
a PFW policy. Most know that the long-range future of their
company is dependent upon the quality of people they hire
today. They know that they must upgrade their present personnel to fill future vacancies. They also know that an employee who does not enjoy a satisfactory growth pattern may
lose his motivation and resign.

Think about it.
Plan ahead.
For many young people, PFW can mean opportunity.

PROBLEM

16

The Preferable Position

Mike was a college dropout who had nevertheless received excellent training in business management while he was enrolled. He was now twenty-two years of age and married. He was considered by his close friends to be a strong leader, highly ambitious, independent, frequently impatient, and easily frustrated.

Mike was interviewed by the Great Western Corporation and the Metropolitan Service Company the same week. After more than two weeks of investigation both companies offered him good jobs. Great Western was a dynamic, risk-taking corporation that made little effort to develop its own people. In fact, it took great delight in hiring top people away from competitive companies. They were interested in Mike primarily because of leadership ability and the fact that he would become immediately productive as an employee. Metropolitan, on the other hand, was a slow, steady company that offered a great deal of security to employees. They had a very firm PFW policy. They liked Mike primarily because of his long-range potential and his ability to get along with people.

Although the starting salary with Great Western was substantially higher, the training program with Metropolitan was superior. *All other significant factors were similar.* Which company do you think Mike should have gone with? What factors should Mike have considered in making his decision? (For suggested answer, see page 211.)

17

"Things sure move slow around here."

Wear Your Patience Suit

The patience suit that most career builders must wear if they are to reach their goals does not usually fit very well. It is poorly tailored to many personalities, especially to the capable, aggressive, and highly motivated individual. Often the suit is uncomfortable to the point of deep frustration. There is no doubt about it: the virtue of patience takes on a new dimension when a person is ambitious and anxious to build a successful career with a large organization. And with good reason.

In the first place, business and industry justifiably seek out the highly ambitious applicant for employment. They want and need dynamic men and women. They want and need people with energy. They want and need the competitive spirit in new employees.

Then, after employment, orientation, and training, it is often necessary to turn around and ask these same people to be patient.

"You are doing great, Joe. Just *wait* for the right opportunity and you'll be off and running."

"Continue to prepare, Heiry—learn all you can in your present job—just *wait*; you'll get your chance."

"It takes time in any organization, Susie. Your day will come. Just sit tight and *wait*. You'll see."

Patience is a virtue that is hard to come by under these circumstances. The patience suit becomes too tight, too confining. It is not all the fault of the individual, for the problem is rooted deeply in our modern culture.

Patience isn't something one learns in school or college. Indeed, the pattern of almost automatic promotions in school is the direct opposite of what is found in the world of work. Through our school systems, people become accustomed to promotions according to age. They start at the first grade and move up to the twelfth and beyond like clockwork—each year a step up, until regular promotions are expected without excessive periods of waiting. Small wonder that some begin to think that life is one progressive step after another whether the step has been truly *earned* or not.

Our society contributes in other ways to this "make it in a hurry" attitude. Both economic and social upward mobility has been the pattern for most Americans in the past few decades. As a result, most young people have been raised in an affluent environment not known previously. So why should they wait around for thirty years to get to the same point? Why should they wait until they're ready to retire to make it, when they might do it by the time they're thirty? Yet when they get their first job, many young people must start at the bottom with a relatively low income, inflationary prices, and no fixed promotion schedule to depend upon. Small wonder that many become impatient and seek shortcuts to better positions and higher incomes.

Large business and industrial organizations do not always have fast promotion schedules, and promotions are not automatic. In the world of business the employee must create his own promotion. He must earn it in the face of wide-open competition from others. There are no guarantees. There are few shortcuts. Each step must be won through high personal productivity and good human relations. It all takes time.

Business and industrial leaders believe in *promotion by merit.*

They know that the opportunity to succeed in open competition with others provides the vitality their organizations must have. Seniority, experience, and age are not always enough to win a given promotion. The new worker can to some degree set his own pattern of promotion, provided that he demonstrates capability.

Promotion by merit is quite different from automatic promotion, and it is when the eager, resourceful employee reaches a plateau that the patience suit becomes more and more uncomfortable. The opportunities to move up still exist—even more than most people realize—but they sometimes come slowly and only after long periods of waiting.

These periods of waiting are critical for the career employee.

They can destroy confidence.

They can create problems.

They can cause needless turnover.

But far more important than all other factors is what can happen to the attitude and productivity of the employee during such periods of waiting. For it is when the career employee going through a plateau period permits his attitude and productivity to drop substantially that he defeats himself. At the very point in his career when he should be working up to his potential, he often slips the most. When this happens, the plateau is often extended by management and others are given the promotional opportunities that exist.

It is not an easy thing to ask an aggressive person to wear a patience suit, but management often has no alternative. Opportunities can and do open up in organizations overnight, but it is almost impossible to produce a steady flow of opportunities to fit the time schedules of individuals.

Management cannot eliminate all of the pressure points that the new employee often faces. Salary schedules cannot be quickly adjusted to the needs of each individual; unexpected family expenses cannot always be taken care of by company insurance programs; there is no way that the organization can take into consideration the standard of living the new employee may have become accustomed to or seeks. A business organization should not be expected to financially accommodate the life styles of all employees.

Management people can, however, understand the frustration that comes when a promising career becomes temporarily bogged down. They know because they have usually been there themselves. They know it is a difficult period. They know it is a time when some begin to question seriously their original occupational goal. They know it is a time when personal values are challenged. They know it is a time when some start to think about returning to college for more formal education.

One large financial organization has actually gone so far as to chart out a leveling off or "wait out" period. They have named it the *big plateau*. New employees in this company usually make steady progress over the first few years, but the big jump from their first supervisory position to junior management often requires a long period of waiting. It may be one, two, three, or more years, because at this level management positions open up very slowly. The problem has become so critical that, once these employees reach the big plateau, the company attempts to provide more counseling to help them over the hump.

Carving out a career inside a large company requires some waiting, even though the patience suit may become most uncomfortable. The very word *career* implies steady progress, not speedy progress.

Being ambitious and capable has never been easy in our society. When a person is in his twenties, a year may seem more like five years. And yet most employees are at least thirty before they have an opportunity to fully demonstrate their true ability.

True, a few people in certain occupational areas find success early. The fields of entertainment, professional sports, sales, and promotional activities, for example, may give the young person with talent, ability, and desire an early breakthrough.

At first, it also appears that the professional person achieves his goal early in life. However, it is easy to forget that those who build careers in medicine, science, law, and the other professions must invest more time in their formal education. The M.D. is often close to thirty when he starts his practice. The same is true for the lawyer, the Ph.D. in physics, and other professionals.

How, then, can the career-minded person who reaches a plateau learn to wear his patience suit better? What can he do to prevent dangerous frustrations and negative attitudes?

He must step back and take the long view of his career potential. He must realize that where he will be in the organization in five years is more important than where he will be next year. He must see his career in perspective. He should ask himself these questions:

- Am I investing my time to the best advantage for my long-range goal with the company?

- Am I taking full advantage of the training opportunities that are available to me *now*?

- Am I keeping sufficiently busy on my present job to avoid being unduly concerned about my future?

- Am I keeping a positive attitude during this critical period of my career?

And after asking himself such questions, he should study and give careful thought to the following three points.

1. The first years with an organization should be viewed by the new employee as training and apprenticeship years, as part of his total educational program. If the career employee receives a good salary and makes progress, he is doing very well indeed. The training and experience he is acquiring must be considered the plus factor during this period. The new employee is serving an internship something like that in the medical profession. All goals that are worth reaching for require some sacrifice. Instant success is seldom in the cards.

2. Many new employees have received a promotion before they were ready, and their careers have been injured permanently. Will you be sufficiently trained for a good opportunity when it does come? Will you really be ready for the responsi-

bility? Will you be sufficiently mature to handle it? "Too much too soon" is a real threat to your long-range goal. Some people throw away their first few years by not taking advantage of their opportunities to learn. If you keep busy learning and improving, you will have less time to be impatient. The first years in any organization are investment years. The dividends you will receive later will be in proportion to the amount you have invested. You cannot afford to wait out your time. You must use every day and make it pay dividends in the future.

3. Although few people question the fact that personal advancement is often slow during the starting years, they seldom point out that the tempo of personal progress can increase greatly in later years. This is one reason why the new worker should not set up a personal timetable for himself. Progress may be slow at the start of your career but very fast later. Set a goal for yourself, yes, but do not expect that goal to arrive exactly according to *your* time schedule. It may not fit that of your organization. If you do set your own time schedule and management is unable to meet it, then you may lose your motivation to excel and this loss will hurt you as well as the company. The future of any company cannot be charted in detail many years in advance. Research, technical changes, market conditions, and many other factors are not predictable. Your job is to be ready when the opportunity occurs—ready and waiting.

Wearing a patience suit gracefully is not easy!

If you understand why you must wear it at times, you will have an advantage over others. And if you wear this suit well, the mangement suit will fit properly when the time comes.

PROBLEM

17

A Danger for Tim

Tim was a tall, handsome, friendly guy who seemed to perform best under a tight and heavy schedule. While a student at his local community college, he carried a full academic load, worked twenty hours each week in a local bank, and led a full social life.

Tim joined a large service-oriented organization at the age of twenty-two. It was a company that had a formal six-month training program for junior executives, and Tim qualified. He spent six months working in different departments. He attended many educational programs that were a part of the training program. After all of this was over, he was assigned as an assistant manager to one of the larger departments. At that time he received a sizable increase in pay and was told that from then on his progress was up to him.

Shortly after assuming his new position, Tim married. He was very happy and settled down to build a successful career for himself. He worked hard for the next eighteen months without receiving a promotion. He thought he was ready to assume more responsibility, and when his wife became pregnant he became more and more anxious about another assignment and an increase in salary. At this point in his career Tim had invested two years with the company. He liked his work. He appreciated the freedom he was given. He was pleased with the personnel policies of the organization and did not question his long-range future. The immediate problem of additional income, however, began to build many pressures inside Tim. He knew that he was on a plateau that would not last forever, but he nevertheless became increasingly impatient.

What, in your opinion, was the greatest danger facing Tim during this plateau period? (For suggested answer, see page 212.)

CHAPTER

18

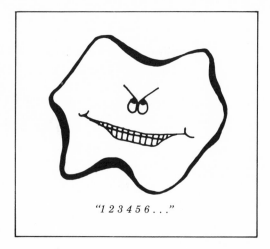

"1 2 3 4 5 6 . . ."

Release
Your Frustrations
Harmlessly

Everyone encounters frustrations in life. We learn to adjust to most of them easily without hurting our relations with others. Sometimes, however, a major frustration or a series of frustrations may cause our feelings to boil to the point where we seriously injure or destroy a relationship we deeply treasure.

Naturally, there are many experiences that occur on the job that are disturbing. In fact, most of your frustrations may be job-oriented. The way you learn to handle these frustrations will influence both the quality of the working relationships you build and your personal progress.

The typist who is in a hurry to get a letter on the desk of her boss suddenly discovers she must change the typewriter

ribbon in order to complete the letter. She suffers a frustration. The mechanic who climbs under a car to do a repair
job, only to discover that he took the wrong wrench with
him, becomes frustrated. The salesperson who writes up an
order in a sales book and then discovers that he forgot to
insert carbon paper naturally feels frustrated.

These little frustrations, as well as more serious ones, come
about when you are trying to reach a goal of some kind and
something happens to slow you down.

A frustration is the inner feeling of disturbance you experience when you meet a temporary block to your immediate
goal.

The more important the goal is to you, the more intense
is the disturbance. Major frustrations come about when something happens to keep you from reaching a goal that means
a great deal to you. While small frustrations can often be
tossed off quickly, major frustrations must often be controlled
for days or weeks until an adjustment can be made. This
can often mean replacing one goal with another.

A good example of this kind of major frustration is the
worker who finds his personal progress with a company too
slow. He has set a goal for himself. He wants to reach a
certain position with his company. He wants to earn a certain
salary. Often in his eagerness he even sets a time schedule
for reaching this goal. He is highly ambitious. His personal
productivity is high, and he is also human relations smart.
He starts to move up the ladder of success.

Then something seems to happen. His progress is temporarily slowed down. His personal time schedule does not agree
with the company's. He feels defeated. His rate of progress
is not according to plan. He has set a goal for himself and
there appears to be a barrier in front of him. What happens?

The situation causes him to become frustrated. He becomes
all stirred up inside. An inner buildup of tensions occurs,
like a steam boiler building up pressure.

Now we must ask ourselves the big question: What happens
when we become frustrated?

Almost always we become aggressive.

The formula is simple. With frustration comes some form
of aggressive behavior. When the steam boiler builds up so

much pressure inside, some of the steam must be released. If there is no safety valve, the boiler will explode. Just as the steam boiler must release some of the pressure after it reaches a certain point, so must the individual. And this release comes usually in some form of aggressive behavior. Aggressive behavior does not always follow frustration. One reason for this might be that we cannot gauge the intensity of the frustration. That is why we refer to the frustration-aggression *hypothesis*. A hypothesis is a kind of premise—an idea. It can never really be proved, but it is enough to work with. Thus, although we can never be certain that aggressive behavior follows frustration of a given intensity, it happens often enough to make it important to understand.

Understanding only the hypothesis is not enough. It is far more important to understand the form that aggressive behavior takes after frustration occurs. There is verbal aggression, and there is physical aggression. Even silence can be a form of aggression.

Take the case of the driver who becomes frustrated when he meets a slow-moving car on the highway. He may say a few unkind words under his breath (verbal aggression) and drive on; he may pound his horn and speed around the slow car (physical aggression); or it could disturb him to the point that when he returns to his office he may not say hello to his secretary as would be his normal custom (silence).

Aggression takes many forms. Releasing some forms of aggression is very dangerous indeed. Physical aggression that involves another person can be assault and battery and could mean a police record. Verbal aggression can also get a person into serious trouble. Telling off a fellow worker or supervisor at the wrong time and wrong place can destroy a relationship and cripple a person's progress for years.

We are all guilty of some physical and some verbal aggressions. Fortunately, most of these are harmless.

The trick is to learn to release our aggressions in acceptable ways. There are acceptable forms of physical aggression. There are acceptable forms of verbal aggression.

A housewife may become frustrated because of her small children. If she acts out the aggression that follows the frustration by overpunishing one child with a very harsh slap in the face, this might be interpreted as an unacceptable release of aggressions. On the other hand, if the mother released her aggressions physically by energetically sweeping out the back porch and then disciplined the child in some other manner, it would be more acceptable. In this case the mother is taking out her aggressions on the porch—not on the child.

There are many acceptable ways in which a person can release inner tensions due to frustrations. Here are a few.

On the job	*Off the job*
Taking a walk	Cooking exotic foods
Talking things over with a third party.	Cleaning out the garage
Doing some disagreeable stock work	Playing golf or going bowling

Sometimes by just physically doing something we release some inner tensions and no one is hurt. It is usually more difficult to find acceptable ways to release inner tensions on the job than it is off the job.

If a worker became frustrated on the job and picked a fight with a fellow worker, this would be an unacceptable release of aggressions. He would be looking for a new job. If, on the other hand, he released his aggressions by walking away and slamming a door where nobody could hear it, he would be releasing his aggressions in an acceptable manner.

Aggressive behavior will not get you into serious trouble unless it hurts people. But aggressive behavior that is socially unacceptable or in poor taste will hurt you in a human relations sense.

In the case above, for example, the young worker would not get into serious trouble if he did not hit his fellow worker. If he released his aggressions by slamming a door in front of many others, he would hurt himself in a human relations sense, because others would interpret the door slamming in an uncomplimentary way. If, however, he held his feelings inside until he could slam a door or walk it off where others were not around, it would not hurt him in any sense.

As a mature, mentally healthy person, you must seek and find acceptable releases for your inner aggressions. You should of course conduct yourself in such a manner as to eliminate as many of the frustrations of life as possible. The fewer frustrations we have, the fewer times we must seek acceptable releases. But one cannot eliminate all frustrations from life. You should expect to find it necessary to release your anxiety feelings occasionally. It is not always healthy for a person to keep his inner tensions bottled up inside. Just as for the steam boiler, some release is necessary.

After a frustrating experience on the job, it is easy to release inner tensions by saying the wrong thing. People who say things that are upsetting to others may be guilty of verbal aggression. They may be saying these things because they have suffered a frustration or series of frustrations and this is a form of release. The inner tensions, caused by a series of frustrations, have reached the boiling point.

Sometimes when a person does not find an acceptable physical release for his feelings, he releases them verbally. Often he does this without knowing it. It is always dangerous. Not that you can control your verbal aggressions one hundred percent of the time. This would be asking too much. But some control is essential.

Sometimes a succession of frustrations causes a more serious inner buildup of pressure. When this happens, some verbal release is necessary. You will do well, however, to refrain from this kind of verbal release to someone on the job. It would be wiser to unburden yourself to someone you can trust outside the organization—your spouse or a good friend, someone who will be a good listener but will not take the matter too seriously and will not pursue it any further.

Here is an illustration that will help you to understand the importance of the frustration-aggression hypothesis.

Alice was intelligent, highly motivated, and well educated. She joined a large utility company as a receptionist. She liked her job, and her productivity and human relations were very good for two years. During this period she took advantage of every opportunity to learn. She received four salary increases. One day, in talking to the personnel director, she mentioned that she would like to qualify as an employment interviewer. The personnel director, pleased with her success so far, encouraged her, saying that she would be considered if an opportunity came along. Alice, more highly motivated than ever, continued to do an outstanding job and set her goal for the next opening in the personnel department.

Two weeks later another young lady was promoted to the personnel department as an interviewer. Alice was not informed about the change. Not thinking that the plans for this personnel change might have been set before her initial talk with the personnel director, Alice permitted herself to become deeply frustrated. She had set a goal for herself and now they had selected another person.

"At least they could have talked to me!"

"Why should *she* get the breaks?"

"So that's the way they keep their promises!"

Alice, without thinking it through, permitted her frustration to grow. Indeed, she set out to feed it, for talking it over with a few fellow employees only intensified her feelings.

What happened?

Alice released her frustration through verbal aggression. For the first time in her career, she sounded off in a weekly staff meeting. She voiced more than her share of gripes during coffee breaks. And all of this found its way back to the personnel department. What was the result? What you might expect: Alice, through her verbal aggression, hurt herself. Six months later another position was open in personnel and Alice was passed over.

What should she have done?

Alice should have released her aggressive behavior outside her job until she discovered the truth of the situation. This would have hurt no one—especially herself. After releasing some of her inner feelings of hostility at home, for instance, she would have become more objective and realized she was in error.

This simple case is just one of many.

Everyone must learn to live with certain frustrating experiences without becoming verbally aggressive on the job, without damaging their relations with others.

Aggressive behavior coming from inner disturbances and hostilities takes many strange forms. It's not always physical or verbal. In extreme cases, aggression takes the form of silence. Deliberate silence. Planned silence.

Silence on the part of the person who has been frustrated is a most potent weapon. Nothing is more uncomfortable to your fellow workers than your silence. No one can interpret your silence. All anyone can do is leave you alone and wait. But it is uncomfortable for them, and productivity suffers.

When a person takes out his inner aggressive feelings in the form of silence, who is at the receiving end? Fellow employees? The supervisor? Although everyone suffers from silence of this nature, the silent person himself suffers the most. He is, in fact, taking out his aggressive feelings on himself. Naturally, this is most destructive to the human personality. It is also juvenile. Many normal, mature people, however, temporarily react to a series of frustrations in this manner.

It is hoped that the preceding discussion has given the reader a good understanding of the frustration-aggression hypothesis. To summarize, how can you put this idea to work for you?

1. If you really understand the idea, you will admit that your frustrations often produce aggressive behavior of some kind and you should learn to recognize this. With this recognition should come the ability to channel aggressive actions into acceptable outlets. Be careful to release your aggressions in the right way and in the right place. Keep from releasing them on the job in a way that will hurt your future.

2. You should be able to recognize quickly aggressive behavior in others. You should then remember that the cause is probably a frustration or series of frustrations. You should not interpret aggressive actions by others as being directed toward you personally. You should accept them as a natural outcome of uncontrollable frustrations. This attitude should make for better human understanding.

3. You should be more sensitive to verbal aggression on your own part and be very cautious in group discussions and staff meetings. When you need to release feelings verbally,

do so to a friend outside the company and not to a fellow employee.

4. You should not let aggressive behavior keep you from reaching your ultimate goal. When a detour is necessary, you should take it. When an unexpected block to your plans appears, accept it for what it is. If frustration occurs, release it in acceptable ways and come up with an alternate goal. Do not allow aggressive behavior to hinder your future.

There is another form of aggression that should be mentioned. It is subtle and· sinister and has been the downfall of many career-minded persons. It is aggression on the part of an employee toward the company he works for. Such a person seems to get along well enough with his fellow workers and immediate supervisors. There is never anything personal about his aggressive behavior—it always seems to be directed toward the company itself. It isn't just the top brass or middle management. It is the company. He often seems to hold his present plight (lack of progress or of personal adjustment to life) against the company. He is the man in the gray flannel suit—with an impersonal target for his aggressions.

In a very real sense it *is* frustrating to work inside any organization. Some rules must be followed. Some degree of conformity is expected. Some loss of individuality is usually necessary. Some people, however, seem to nurse their minor frustrations into one major hang-up against the organization itself. When this is permitted to happen, aggressive action of serious proportions frequently develops. The employee begins to fight a hypothetical monster that seems to be controlling his life without giving him a chance to change. Often one hears expressions like these from such an individual:

"This outfit does nothing but chew people up and spit them out."

"This company is so large that the only thing that keeps us from getting lost altogether is the payroll department."

"I'd put in for a transfer but by the time it got through channels I'd be ready to retire."

These expressions are, in effect, manifestations of frustrations. The search for personal identity and recognition becomes difficult because of the sheer magnitude of the company itself.

This is the same kind of frustration that overcomes a person living in a highly populated metropolitan area. Society is complex today. So are large organizations. Nobody is to blame personally, so the individual decides to take out his aggressions on the company itself. Just as one does not fight society and still find success within its framework, so it is with a large company.

You just don't fight a large company—and win! In the first place, it is too large for one person to fight. Second, there is no way to fight it and survive within it. Third, when one fights a company he eventually loses his loyalty to it.

And it begins to show. Not overnight, of course. But it shows in subtle ways that begin to hurt the progress of the individual. To build a successful career inside a big organization one must not become so frustrated that he tries to take it out on the company itself.

This chapter has given you a simple idea—an idea that will help you understand yourself and others better. It is called the frustration-aggression hypothesis. It is, in a way, a warning.

Give it some thought.

PROBLEM

18

The Frustrated Engineer

It took Victor three months to make up his mind to join the new company. His decision to do so was based primarily upon the promise that they would push him ahead as fast as he could take it. The previous two engineering concerns he had worked for had never given him the opportunity to move ahead at a pace that was satisfying to him. Vic's wife claimed that he always set impossible goals for himself, and that he would never be completely satisfied.

Everything went well for the first six months on his new job. Then one day Vic discovered that an engineer, far less experienced than he, had been was promoted. This caused him to wonder whether he had been oversold on the opportunities that were available for him. He started to check on the progress of other engineers. He kept saying to himself, "Well, I'll give them a year and if nothing happens I'm going to start looking elsewhere."

Shortly before Vic had completed a full year with the company, he was told he would be transferred to another plant some thirty miles away. He became very excited about the transfer. He knew it would mean a big promotion for him. On reporting to work at the new plant, however, he discovered that the personnel officer was cool and noncommittal toward him and he was given a position that appeared to have less responsibility than the one he had left. Having built up his hopes, Vic felt let down. Then other things happened. He soon learned that his living expenses were higher in the new location. His wife claimed that the schools were not as good. One negative thing after another happened until Vic became increasingly frustrated After three weeks in the new assignment, he walked into the personnel department one afternoon and explosively released his feelings. He shouted. He ranted. He pounded the table.

Halfway through the outburst the personnel officer said: "Slow down. Take it easy. Cool off. Relax." Then he proceeded to read a letter just received from the home office announcing that Vic was to replace a man who had just received a promotion himself. It was a big jump.

Was Vic justified in his outburst? What might he have done to prevent it? Did he harm himself permanently, even though he did receive the promotion? (For suggested answer, see page 214.)

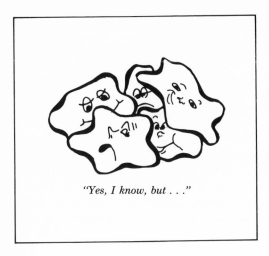

"Yes, I know, but . . ."

Meet Joe Harvey Again

You will remember Joe from an earlier chapter. Here he comes again!

"Good morning, Joe. What's on your mind?"

"Well, I have been doing some serious thinking since I started to read this book about human relations. I believe that I now sense my human relations responsibilities and opportunities, but a few things bother me at this point. So if you have time I'd like to ask some questions."

For example, how can I keep a positive attitude when my job is boring?

Good question, Joe. People are usually bored for either of two reasons. First, there may be little or no activity connected with the job. The work load may drop temporarily, or, as in the case of a retail store, few customers may show up during slow periods. The second reason is that the work itself may be boring. This is especially true of jobs that are repetitive or routine—jobs that never offer a new challenge, or so it seems.

In the case of inactivity, the employee must manufacture work to keep a positive attitude. He must use his initiative to find work—*any* work—during slow periods. Inactivity on the job will give a person a negative attitude every time, and the only way to fight it is to find something to do. Something constructive!

The matter of having a job that does not consistantly provide sufficient excitement or personal challenge is another kind of problem. Those who have lived through some boring jobs claim that they have had to *make* them interesting. They experiment in doing the job in different ways. They play games with themselves to keep up their interest. In other words, they look at the positive side of the job. Boredom is a sinister emotion. It can destroy your positive attitude and sap your enthusiasm without your knowing it. And once you become bored, it is like being in a deep pit—it takes time to get out. Because this is true, challenge yourself from the very start. If you do this, boredom will not become a major problem and you will keep the positive attitude you started out with.

Whom should I turn to if I run into a human relations problem I can't handle myself?

If you have analyzed the problem carefully and made repeated attempts to solve it yourself without noticeable success, there are many people you can turn to for assistance. The important thing is that you go to *somebody*. It is important that you talk over these problems and not keep them inside until they grow out of proportion and damage your career. Time itself does not always solve human problems, and when your productivity and that of others are being impaired, action is often necessary.

Normally, your immediate supervisor is the person to see. In some cases, someone in the personnel department might be better. It is important to go to someone whom you respect and who is receptive. It is also important to go to someone who will discuss the problem in confidence. If there is no one inside the company you honestly feel you can consult, your only alternative is to talk with an outsider. If this is the case, be sure the person will keep the problem under his hat. It is of course always better not to identify personalities. Try to present the problem in a fair and objective manner without building too much of a case for yourself. Remember, it takes two to create a human relations problem. Seldom is any problem entirely the fault of *one* person. Talking over a problem with the right person may not solve it, but it can give you a perspective that may help you solve it. It can lower the pressure that has been building and give you some new insights into human understanding.

What do you do when you feel your immediate supervisor is strongly prejudiced against you?

If you have received an excessive amount of harrassment or unfair treatment over an extended period of time, and you are absolutely certain that some form of prejudice (racial or otherwise) exists, you should gather up your courage and take the following three steps in sequence.

1. Arrange a face-to-face discussion with your supervisor in private as soon as possible. It will be difficult to do, but state your feelings openly and frankly. In doing this don't accuse or needlessly antagonize him or her by your attitude or words. Once you have stated your case, listen carefully to his side of the story. Should he disclaim any feelings of conscious or subconscious prejudice toward you, accept him at his word and do your level best to improve the relationship during the next few weeks.

2. If the relationship does not improve in the next few weeks, go to your personnel officer or a higher manager (your supervisor's boss) and ask for a two- or three-way

discussion (including the supervisor) of the problem. As in your previous confrontation, state your case to the best of your ability and continue to be a good listener. Whatever happens as a result of this meeting, try not to be hostile or vindictive toward the supervisor or the company.

3. If the relationship still does not improve and the harassment and unfair treatment continues, formally request a transfer and at the same time start looking for a position with another company. There is no justifiable reason why you should continue to work under a supervisor guilty of prejudice toward you.

Isn't it possible that if you are too human relations smart your co-workers might become envious and as a result you might do more harm than good?

This can happen only when the individual overplays his human relations hand. A person who is truly human relations smart is graceful, skillful, sincere, and natural in building relationships with others. He is not obvious to the point where co-workers would know about it and become envious.

How do you get through to someone who is human relations dumb?

Everyone is human relations dumb at times, so in a sense we all need all of the help we can get. In rare instances, it might be possible for you to help a close friend or co-worker improve his human relations approach in building better relationships with others, providing the individual *wants* your help. Helping those people who seem to constantly foul up their relationships with others (or those who reject them), however, is a risky business and should, usually, be left to those who are professionally trained in counseling or therapy. The cause may be deeper than you think, and your best approach in these situations is to be satisfied in building the best possible relationship with them even though they may not respond as you feel they should. Not all people, of course, can be helped even by the professionals.

Can a person be formally trained to be more sensitive to the needs of others and, as a result, understand himself better and become more human relations smart?

A great deal of experimental work is going on today in this area. Many different kinds of sensitivity and encounter groups are being conducted both on and off campuses in America. Whether such sessions are helpful or harmful to the individual depends on many complicated factors, the most important of which is the professional background, skill, and sensitivity of the leader himself. Should you receive an invitation to participate in such a group, you would be wise to base your acceptance upon whether or not it is sponsored by a reliable organization and conducted by a truly professional person.

What if I should get stuck in an assignment with no future? How do I go about getting a transfer?

This is a difficult question to answer, Joe. Every organization has its own procedure. You must always respect local ground rules. Most transfers are handled through personnel departments with full communication with management and department heads. A request of this nature should go through normal channels and, if possible, should be made on a face-to-face basis with or without a written statement.

It is never human relations smart to act prematurely on transfer requests. If you do, you might communicate to others that you can't handle the job or that you can't take a difficult, temporary assignment. Some starting jobs, for example, are traditional stages in a career, and everyone must sweat them out. Under these conditions, an early request can hurt you.

What action should I take if I find myself in a position for which I am overqualified?

It is not unusual for a very bright or highly educated person to start a career from an entry position that does not come close to fully using his or her potential. Sometimes such a job is the only one available. In such a situation, it is usually to the individual's advantage to live with the job—

do it well and keep a positive attitude—until something
more challenging opens up. In other words, the best action
may be to sweat it out. If you find yourself in such a
position, Joe, there are two factors you should keep in mind.

1. Should you communicate to others, through your attitude, that you feel you are too good for the job, you may
damage your relations with them and perhaps postpone
the day when you will receive more of a challenge.

2. Your best approach would be to try and make your job
bigger than it now is. In other words, assume more responsibility as opportunities arise. Without hurting your relationships with others, demonstrate your ability in different
ways, such as forwarding well-researched suggestions
through the proper channels, asking to make certain improvements in procedures, or simply doing something others
have neglected. If you take this approach you will keep
management aware of your potential in a positive way,
and chances are good they will then make better use of
it sooner.

Should you find yourself inside an organization that cannot
make good use of your special potential, you should make
a switch as soon as possible. A job that temporarily doesn't
use your potential is one thing; a company that can't use
it is another.

*When and how should I go about asking for a raise or a
salary adjustment?*

Salary hang-ups between an employee and management
can create human relations havoc, so it is obvious that
you have asked another touchy question that is difficult
to answer. Don't start out anticipating any problems, because it may never be necessary for you to ask for a raise
or adjustment. The great majority of these are made without request. There are circumstances, however, when action on your part might be necessary and advisable. For
example, you might have been promised an increase that
did not materialize on time. A pleasant reminder could
quickly clear up the oversight.

You might also find yourself in the position where you feel disturbed because you are doing the same job as others but your pay is less, or you have waited longer than they have for an increase, or your job needs to be reclassified. If you begin to feel this way you are encouraged to do something about it, but don't jump too fast with too little. Do you have the facts straight? Have you fully demonstrated your superior productivity over a substantial period of time? Has your responsibility really increased? Are there other factors involved?

You should not, of course, be afraid of going to management to discuss your salary problems. If it is important to you, it is also important to them. The longer you wait and nurse the problem the more disturbed and negative you will become. *Salary problems destroy positive attitudes and productivity and must be reconciled as soon as possible.* But you should go about it in the right way to avoid making a serious human relations mistake. Try not to carry a chip on your shoulder. Try not to build a case for yourself ahead of time and then aggressively try to prove your point without listening to the other side. A salary discussion, like other discussions, should provide two-way communication that will solve the problem. It should not be a bargaining hassle in which deep hostilities develop—hostilities that are often irreconcilable. After all, your goal should be to get a fair adjustment and at the same time not injure your relations with management. It is not human relations smart to cut off your future to gain immediate satisfaction in a relatively small matter.

Why do we need good human relations with people we may never see again and who therefore can't help us in business?

There are two basic reasons why you should practice good human relations with *everybody* you meet, both on and off the job. The first reason is very practical; the second is philosophical. First, you just can't tell whether or not you will ever meet another person a second time. People have a way of showing up in strange places. If you mistreat or ignore a person when you first meet him, you may pay a high price at a later date. Second, practicing good human relations should become a way of life, Joe, not just something you can turn on or off based upon what it can do for you. You must believe that the people at the other end of relationships are important and worth the best treatment you can provide. Unless you really feel this way, you are only playing a game, and your human relations endeavors will most likely be interpreted as surface gestures. As a result, your relationships with others will be very shallow.

My girl friend is attractive and very out-going. How can she build healthy relationships with highly competitive women who have tendencies toward jealousy?

This is a giant order because perceptive people will usually agree that most pretty women, unless they are very human relations smart, can easily attract hostility from other women. The cause? There appears to be an emotionally seated competitive element inside some women that drives them to challenge those females who are rather well physically endowed, sexually attractive to men, excellent in their jobs, and who are *also* competitive. The tactics in these subtle little wars are one hundred percent female, sometimes even vicious, and unless there is a big blow-up, men seldom know they are going on.

The best thing your girl friend could do would be to never let the problem occur in the first place. In other words, when she starts out on a job she should use every good human relations technique and principle she knows to build good relationships before there is a chance for jealousy and hostility to set in. In doing this, she should keep in mind that although good relations with men are also important, she should concentrate, on her female relationships if she is to avoid the problem. The moment most women discover that another female is spending her time building male relationships, the problem comes to the surface.

What should she do if the problem develops anyway and

she finds herself on the receiving end of some unfair treatment? Here are a few suggestions.

1. It is easy to say and hard to do, but she should try not to take it too personally. Another attractive girl in her place might receive the same hostile treatment. The worst thing she could do would be to fight back in kind, because nothing would please the other party more than to get "to her."

2. She should be her natural self and yet try to minimize the problem by conducting herself in a very business like manner. She should not play up to men or let them give her too much special attention. She should endeavor to keep her body language somewhat subdued. She should dress herself down slightly. She should not permit another woman to intimidate her; on the other hand, it is not smart to deliberately provoke hostility by one's own behavior.

3. In extreme cases, a friendly face-to-face discussion of the matter over a cup of coffee might help. Even relationships loaded with hostility can improve if enough communication takes place and a common ground for respect is found.

Those who have seriously considered the matter will recognize two other factors that are sometimes involved. One, the problem is often compounded when the woman in question occupies a key position in an organization, such as that of secretary to a top executive. Two, the problem would be far less prevalent if all women would subscribe to the idea that in the world of work everyone should be judged upon his or her productivity and not personal matters. Prejudice takes many forms, and a woman who becomes jealous of another because of her female charms, and not what she contributes to the organization, is not only being unfair but also human relations dumb. Such behavior does not go unnoticed, and she is probably hurting herself more than she suspects.

If you are human relations smart but your supervisor is not, how do you go about using your human relations ability to get you where you want to go?

I expected this question, Joe, and I don't mind saying that it is very difficult to answer, especially if you are working for such a supervisor now and your job and the company are important to you. You'll have to decide whether or not to stick it out, but here are a few things to think about.

Chances are good you won't be stuck with such a supervisor for long, so view your experience as temporary. Almost everyone in upper management has had to sweat it out under a difficult supervisor sometime in his life. Do not permit the situation to force you to resort to poor human relations moves yourself. Try to build a good human relations reputation despite your uncomfortable situation. Study the mistakes your supervisor makes, and make sure you don't someday incorporate them into your own leadership style. You should also be generous enough to keep in mind that being a supervisor is probably more difficult than you suspect. When you get there, you may not be as good a manager as you think. Almost all supervisors have good qualities. Only a very few are as human relations dumb as their employees think. You can also afford to be a little generous, because you may have had the opportunity for more training in human relations than your supervisor has.

How do you maintain good human relations when trying to rebuff advances from a member of the opposite sex who is in your department, especially if it is your supervisor?

Everyone must do this in his or her own way, of course, but if you can manage to be gracious but firm in front of others in the department, you might not only build better relations with them but you might solve the problem itself.

How can you build good horizontal relations with others when they know you are a good personal friend of the manager because of a previous relationship?

It is a tough thing to live through, but the following will

help. (1) Keep your relations with this person on a strict business basis while on the job. (2) Do not take advantage of the relationship in any manner or form and concentrate on keeping your personal productivity above reproach. (3) Work harder at your horizontal relationships so that your co-workers will eventually respect you for yourself and your contribution and not because you know the manager personally.

How do you handle a situation in which two of your co-workers have a very strong dislike for each other, and you are in the middle?

Stay in the middle and do the best you can. Both relationships are equally important to you and to the productivity of the department, so you must try not to side with one or the other and contribute to a possible split in the department. Your best bet is to try to keep both relationships strong and healthy. If you side with one person you automatically hurt your relationship with the other, and it is always possible that the person you side with may resign and leave you holding the bag, or the person you turn away from may become your supervisor. There is nothing to keep you from trying to resolve the problem, but you should understand the risks involved and remember that your supervisor probably knows what is going on and could take action from a better position than yours, should he or she want to.

What if I should discover a fellow employee being dishonest? What responsibility do I have to the company?

You ask good questions, Joe. This is a hard one to answer, because your company may have a policy you should follow. Before taking action you should see if such a policy exists.

Your question assumes that you discover an act of dishonesty by a fellow employee. We hope that this doesn't happen, because it will put you in a very uncomfortable position. But if it does, you do have a responsibility to your company. You also have a responsibility to yourself.

One possible procedure is to go to the employee directly and tell him that you noticed a certain incident, and that you will feel obliged to go to management should you observe such an incident again. This is not easy to do. You must be careful of your facts. You should never accuse. Just say that you observed.

If this approach seems inadvisable, your only alternative is to report the incident to the best of your ability to a responsible person who will honor your confidence and start an investigation. Whatever happens after that is not your responsibility. Dishonesty is a touchy business. You must protect yourself from involvement and at the same time carry out your responsibility as an employee. An on-the-spot accusation should be avoided at all costs. Evidence is hard to come by, and getting it should be left to the experts.

Do I have a public relations responsibility to my company?

The image your company has in the mind of the public has a great influence on the company's success. So the answer to your question is yes. Of course, if you have contact with customers, public relations is part of your job. You are paid to work well with customers. If you have no on-the-job contacts with the public, you still have a public relations responsibility. The image of your company can be hurt around the bridge table, on the golf course, or through many other contacts you may have.

It may seem old-fashioned to you, Joe, but keeping certain problems and discussions within the company family is human relations smart. As long as you accept employment with a company, you are an insider and you share in the responsibility to communicate a good image to outsiders. It is *your* company. If you downgrade it in any way to your friends, you are in effect downgrading yourself.

Is too much conformity demanded in a large organization? Must I lose my individuality to build a career?

This is a very good question, and one that is being asked

more and more often. Some very popular books have recently dealt with this problem. It must be admitted that a certain amount of conformity is necessary in working for a company. But isn't this also true of our culture in general? Isn't it true, at least to some extent, in community life? Isn't it also true in social organizations?

Remember the chapters in the book that dealt with building good horizontal and vertical working relationships? You will recall it was suggested that some degree of conformity would be necessary. *Some* conformity does not mean you will lose your identity. Your company does not want you to become a carbon copy of other people. It does not want you to become a face in the crowd. You will lose some of your value to the company if you do. It is important that you become a good working member of the company and still keep your individuality. The most basic of all human relations principles is recognition of individual differences. It is human relations smart to be different. Over-conformity is as dangerous as nonconformity. The line between is a tightrope all employees walk. To be a strong working member of a group and still maintain individuality is no easy trick.

PROBLEM

A Plan for Lupe

Lupe was a beautiful young lady with a trim figure and a flare for wearing the right clothes in the right way. She was also very bright (almost a straight A average in school), and she was determined to be successful. Lupe had married in her first year in college, so she had to drop out. She had intended to be an English major. Her marriage hadn't made it, so she was living with her mother. Lupe had a one-year-old daughter whom she loved dearly.

She took a job working in the editorial department of a rather large publishing concern. Her position was classified as a general office clerk and typist. She worked under four editors, three of whom were female. The pay was good. The hours and location were great. Besides, it was the best job she could find under the circumstances.

Everything went beautifully for a while. It wasn't long, however, before two things began to bother Lupe. First, the job itself became a drag. The typing was easy. The filing was boring. It was all too routine and just did not challenge her potential enough. Besides, she was certain she could do a better job of editing than some of the editors. She also thought she could get along well with the art department, coming up with creative ideas to improve manuscripts, and many other things that only editors could do. The other matter that started getting to Lupe was the hostility she could sense coming from a few of the other women around the office, especially from one of the female editors she worked for. Sure, Lupe knew she was pretty and that she attracted attention. Some of the men around the organization made passes at her. But she couldn't see what was wrong with being the kind of person she really was. Besides, she did superior work, and that was what she had been hired for in the first place.

What kind of a human relations course or plan do you think Lupe should have followed? What would have made it possible for her to move into a more challenging position with the blessings and support of the other women in her department? (For suggested answer, see page 214.)

CHAPTER

20

"Things always look better on the outside."

When Other Pastures Look Greener

Freedom to accept or resign a job, seek employment in a special occupational area, or join an organization of one's choice is an important American freedom. It should be appreciated by all free people. But what does it really mean to you?

It means that you can leave a position with a large or small organization and go into business for yourself; it means you can leave any occupation and go back to school to continue your education; it means you can leave one company and join another. It means that you can keep on leaving one company for another until you find the job, occupational area, or company you desire.

Some resignations are soundly planned and are best for the organization and the individual. Some resignations, for a variety of personal reasons, are unavoidable. Some, however, seem to stem from poor judgment and turn out to be mistakes.

There are of course certain dangers to any resignation, so you should be cautious and objective in making such a move. If you make a mistake, you may lose an investment in time, effort, and experience that you can never fully regain elsewhere. You may wind up with a job that is not as good as the one you left. You might even wind up temporarily stranded. Thousands of people leave organizations every year only to regret it later. The pastures in another occupational area or company may, from a distance, look greener than they really are. Resigning a position, whether you have a door open elsewhere or not, is a serious move.

When, then, should you resign a position?

As a general rule, you should resign when you have been *unhappy and unproductive for a considerable length of time.* Under such conditions you have in all probability had a negative attitude for a long time and, as a result, your career with the company has already been seriously damaged. A new start in a new environment would most likely be to your advantage.

Young people who are ambitious should look elsewhere for employment when they discover they have not been living close to their potential for a long time; they should seek opportunities elsewhere when their productivity has been down for months, and they can't get it back up; they should consider other options when their attitudes have been negative for a long stretch and they do not seem to be able to do anything about it.

Surveys and statistics show, however, that most resignations are not due to the above reasons, *but are based primarily upon personality conflicts and human problems.* Because such problems can frequently be solved or at least made less traumatic, it would appear that many people resign their positions for the wrong reasons. In other words, leaving a job because it is not the *right* one for you is one thing, but leaving a job because of human problems that you might solve or continue to find elsewhere is something else.

To help you avoid these and other mistakes, here are five questions to ask yourself when considering a resignation.

1. Are you resigning under emotional stress?

Everyone is tempted to chuck a job when everything seems to be going wrong and one becomes deeply frustrated and emotionally upset. It is a natural reaction. A resignation, however, should be a rational decision based upon many facts, including what other opportunities are available, and should be made only after long and careful analysis and planning. It is difficult to think clearly and logically when you are emotionally disturbed about a problem that cannot be quickly solved, so during these periods back away from such a serious decision. Sleep on it. Talk to a third person. Give it time. A resignation should not be an impulsive decision, because in the majority of cases it is irrevocable.

2. Have you talked your situation over with your supervisor or the person who employed you?

Many employees are fearful of talking over a possible resignation with a management person because they think they might be terminated immediately and it would hurt their chances of finding a better job elsewhere. Some feel it would be an act of disloyalty. Others feel it to be a waste of time. Whatever your reason, you would be smart not to resign until *after* you discuss the problem with your supervisor or someone in personnel. A twenty-minute discussion with the right person has stopped many a foolish resignation. Many problems can be resolved through free and open communication with management. Give those in charge a chance to resolve your problem before you take final action. You have nothing to lose, and you may discover that the position you are thinking of leaving has more potential than any you could find elsewhere.

3. Are you resigning because of a personality conflict?

Resigning because of a single personality is a shortsighted way to build a lifelong career. This is not to say that such conflicts cannot be serious. They can be. But they can usually be resolved with time and effort. Give someone in authority a chance to help. Give time a chance to help. Most of all, be honest with yourself and ask whether you can afford to let one person destroy a promising career—especially when it is *yours.*

4. Are you resigning to save face?

Everyone makes mistakes, and sometimes you may over-commit yourself or take a stand on an issue that you feel you cannot back away from. A resignation becomes the easy way out. You cannot stay and save face. Resigning on this basis can be a mistake, especially if you have exaggerated the difficulty of the adjustment. It may be better to admit a mistake than to pay a price out of all proportion, particularly when such a resignation might be harmful to both your future and the company's.

5. Are you living close to your potential?

Your future depends on your having a position in a company where you can work close to your potential. You must be able to use your ability, aptitudes, and talents to a reasonable extent. You must be productive to succeed. You must find a way to contribute. *Your company is entitled to the best you.* If you find your position doesn't bring out the best in you, then it isn't fair to either you or the company for you to remain. You should find something more suitable, because an employee who is not productive is doing himself and his company more harm than good.

If after serious consideration of all the above questions you decide to resign in the best interests of both parties, how should you go about it? Here are a few tips on how to resign gracefully.

Resign on a face-to-face basis. Always go to the person who employed you as well as to your supervisor and resign face to face. A letter of resignation or a telephone resignation alone will always leave a bad impression. It may hurt you later on when another organization wants a reference. You will gain the respect of management when you resign in person. You will feel better too.

Tell management the real reason for your resignation. It is important that a business organization know the real reasons employees resign. Reliable information can lead to changes that will benefit all. If you are honest with management, they will understand you better and your status as a former employee will be improved. Honesty is always the best human relations policy.

Give ample notice. Be sure that you give at least the traditional two weeks notice. This amount of time may be necessary for the company to recruit and train a replacement.

Continue to be productive. Don't take advantage of the fact that you are leaving. You will gain respect from others as well as personal satisfaction by working hard up to the very last hour. This is one way to leave a clean record behind you.

Turn in all equipment. All company equipment, down to the most minute item, should be officially turned in through regular channels.

Transfer all responsibilities to your replacement gracefully. Give the person taking over your job a break. Give him all possible help and assistance. Try not to leave him with any problems you can take care of before leaving. Transfer to him as far as possible any good relationships you have developed.

Swallow any last-minute negative comments. There is a temptation, after resignation, for some people to become negative and pour out their hostilities. It is especially important not to transfer your negative attitudes to your replacement. Give him a chance to make his own adjustment without sour notes from you.

Say goodbye when you go. Be sufficiently courteous to say goodbye personally to all who have helped you. If you are unable to see someone, send him a note.

Always resign a position in such a manner that you will feel free to seek reemployment at a later date. It is human relations smart to do so.

You are the sum total of all your experiences. Should you ever find it necessary to sever your affiliation with a company, you would not leave empty-handed. You would take your experience and training with you. And you would of course take the knowledge you've gained from your human relations mistakes with you. And such knowledge is never without value.

In closing, it should also be mentioned that sometimes business and governmental organizations find it necessary to terminate the services of employees because of economic reasons beyond their control. There is, therefore, a remote possibility that you may someday be involved in a layoff, cut-back, or furlough situation. Should this happen it is obvious that some of the tips above are applicable. Here are three more that might help you during such an adjustment period.

1. Remember that it is not your fault or the company's, so it is a waste of time to blame anyone.
2. It does not hurt your reputation to be caught in such a situation. You can and should continue to be proud of your record.
3. It is bad enough to lose your job; but if you lose your positive attitude along with it, you are a double loser.

PROBLEM

20

Too Late with Too Little?

If you had known Mark in college you would have thought of him as a great guy. He was easy to know, fun to be around, and a real tease. Although he was far from the top in his class academically, he was possibly the best known.

Because of his friendly personality and positive attitude toward life, Mark found it easier to get a good job after graduation than most of his classmates, even though most of them had much better records. After looking into a number of possibilities, he joined a large manufacturing concern on the east coast close to his family. After three years he had made little progress. In fact, most of his classmates had far out-distanced him as far as responsibility and income were concerned. Why? After a careful analysis based upon a long talk with the personnel director, Mark admitted to himself that he had hurt his own progress because of the following: (1) he had been a little naïve about the importance of human relations and, as a result, he had made a few serious mistakes that would be hard to live down; (2) his personal productivity had gone down during the last year; (3) he had, at least to some extent, lost his positive attitude toward the job, the company, and his career.

Mark still thought he had joined a fine company. He liked most of their policies. Both he and his wife thought the geographical area was great, and they did not want to move. He did not know of another good position or company, but he knew he could find one if the chips were down.

Should Mark have resigned and searched for a better opportunity, or should he have tried to make up for his mistakes in the past, regain his positive attitude, and stick with it? (For suggested answer, see page 215.)

Suggested Answers to Case Problems

The human relations problems presented at the end of each chapter in this book were designed to be springboards for individual thinking and discussion purposes *only*. The reader is cautioned that, unlike mathematics problems, they have no exact answers. The reasons are obvious.

In the first place, each problem is incomplete in that it presents only a few facts, and without *all* the facts anything approaching a definite or complete answer would be dangerous indeed. Also, different points of view are always possible (even encouraged) in discussions of human relations problems.

The following so-called answers, then, are nothing more than the author's opinion of how he would approach the problem with the available facts. They should serve only as a guide to the independent thinking of the reader and the discussion leader.

PROBLEM

1

"It's <u>who</u> you know that counts."

Rod Faces Reality

It is easy, at first reading, to understand why Rod was disturbed because the two others received promotions ahead of him. Rod's pride was hurt because he had worked hard and efficiently at his specific job. But there is at least some evidence that points to the possibility that he was trying to escape his full human relations responsibility. Did he make *enough* effort to cooperate and build good relationships with his co-workers? Was he sufficiently tolerant? Did he put everything into efficiency at the expense of human relations?

The author believes that Rod was not fully justified in saying "It isn't what you know but who you know that counts." It appears that he might have been using an old cliché as a rationalization to justify his unwillingness to make more of an effort in building better relationships. He was reminded twice by his supervisor to be more a part of the group. He did not take the hint. It would therefore appear that Rod felt his job depended ninety-eight percent on his personal productivity and only two percent on human relations. He did not see why he had more of a responsibility to work closely with others in his department in order to help *their* productivity.

The case of Rod was designed to point out that an ambitious employee who works hard and efficiently is not always human relations smart. Few people can neglect human relations and still make their full contribution to the productivity of their department.

PROBLEM

2

"What's wrong with my personality?"

The Case of Miss Katy

Katy probably would have to make some concessions before she could find another job where she could be fully happy. She failed to understand that when she was aloof, distant, and hostile she was uncomfortable to work next to; she failed to comprehend that her fellow workers might have needed to communicate with her on a friendly basis whether she needed to communicate with them or not. A sound, healthy working relationship is a two-way thing, and Katy would have to learn to relax and give a little more of herself if she wanted to find an environment in which she could be happy and productive. It is doubtful whether she could ever make her maximum contribution to her job and company as long as she stayed so deeply inside her shell and expected others to come to her. Katy may have been extremely sensitive about going half-way in building relationships because she had been rejected or hurt in the past and, as a result, did not have the personal confidence to reach out and start a sound working relationship. If she made the effort to discover that most people are not only easy to know but *worth* knowing, she would have confidence and adjust more easily to all new environments.

PROBLEM

3

"It's hard to stay positive."

Manuel's Changing Attitude

It is questionable that one can pinpoint the very day when a major change in attitude takes place, so it would be a hasty judgment to agree with Manuel that he should have resigned his job a year ago. Of course, now that it is over, Manuel has the benefit of hindsight to help him assess his unhappy experience. Although changes in attitude usually creep up on a person rather slowly, Manuel should have tested himself when he discovered that his enthusiasm was down over a period of a few weeks. Was it the job itself that was responsible? Was it a conflict over his own personal career desires? Was it his own immaturity? Manuel should have taken an honest inventory of himself and his job much earlier. He should have talked to his manager or perhaps a professional counselor outside.

If he came to the conclusion that his values and desires were not in harmony with the job, he should have started to look elsewhere or considered going back to school. If, however, the job itself was not the major cause of his negative attitude, then he should have made more of an effort to regain his positive attitude. It is not fair to one's self or one's company to drift along over a lengthy period of time with a very negative attitude, especially when the individual is young and does not have heavy family responsibilities.

Manuel refused to be honest with himself in evaluating the change and the cause of the change in his attitude, and as a result he made neither a big effort to be positive again nor a serious effort to find another career opportunity. He just drifted along in an unhappy and unproductive state until he was terminated. In doing this, he not only lost valuable time, but he also hurt his future because a voluntary resignation is always better on one's record than a forced termination.

PROBLEM

4

"My supervisor ignores me."

The Aloof Supervisor

If Bernie had decided to concentrate on horizontal working relationships he would have made a safe and sound move, but for him to concentrate on them exclusively should be questioned. No matter how unapproachable a supervisor may be, one should continue to try and build a relationship with him or her. The fact that others in the department had apparently failed did not mean that Bernie would.

He should have continued to wait and watch for opportunities. He should have worked hard. He should have sent out friendly signals. He should have made suggestions for improvements, if they were well thought out. He should have occasionally forced a conversation. One should never give up on a difficult relationship or build one at the expense of another. Bernie could easily have made a mistake by putting all of his human relations eggs in the horizontal basket.

PROBLEM

5

"Now you tell me . . ."

Jeff Misses the Message

The author goes along with the decision to pass over Jeff for the supervisory position based upon the following reasons.

1. It would be a natural reaction for Jeff's co-workers to resent him as a supervisor because he failed to build good horizontal working relationships with them when he had the chance. If they resent him, productivity may drop steeply under his leadership.

2. An individual who doesn't learn how to build good horizontal relationships as an employee will probably have trouble building good vertical relationships as a supervisor.

3. A supervisor achieves greater departmental productivity more from building good relationships than from the work he actually performs himself. Consequently, Jeff was a poor risk as a supervisor.

By neglecting his horizontal working relationships when he first joined the department, Jeff made a classic human relations mistake. The price he must pay could be high. Perhaps someone from personnel should have a series of counseling sessions with him on the fundamentals of good human relations in an attempt to save him for management. If he continues to miss the message, his career as a manager may never get off the ground.

PROBLEM

6

"Okay, next time I'll cool it . . ."

The Unhappy High Producer

Although Ted's impatience and exasperation are understandable, the supervisor had a point and was right in counseling him to keep his cool and not further damage his horizontal relationships. Ted was well along the way to becoming a supervisor, and had he continued to be critical of others he might have forfeited his opportunity. It should be pointed out, however, that Ted was in a tough spot. It is extremely difficult to maintain personal productivity above co-workers and still keep good relations with them. If Ted really wanted to be the next supervisor, this was the price he would have to pay.

The supervisor was wrong in not giving Ted the recognition he deserved sooner. He was also wrong in not counseling Ted before he became frustrated and damaged his horizontal relationships. Ted must learn, however, that few supervisors are perfect and that he must protect his future by playing it human relations smart even when his supervisor is at fault.

PROBLEM

7

"I'm a Theory Y person myself."

A Choice in Supervisors

You have an intriguing but difficult choice. The older, Theory X supervisor might give you the following advantages: (1) he has been with the company longer and has had more experience, so he might be able to teach you more; (2) he probably knows more management people at the top, so if you can gain his respect he might be able to push you along faster; (3) although he may demand more from you, in the long run you might be a stronger person and eventually a better supervisor yourself because of it.

If you choose the younger, Theory Y supervisor, you might enjoy the following advantages: (1) chances are good you would become more involved under his leadership and, as a result, become more productive and happier; (2) he may be more up to date in his leadership style, so you might better prepare yourself for a leadership role by working under him; (3) it looks like he'll move up the management ladder soon, so perhaps if you work hard you can take his place soon and move even higher later on because of his influence from above.

Your answer to the problem should be based upon the following factors:

1. In which work environment would you be the happiest and most productive?
2. How would your personality and your values make it with each supervisor?
3. How ambitious are you to get into management?

Obviously, both supervisors would provide certain advantages and certain disadvantages. If you understand their leadership styles in advance, you should be able to make the best decision. Neither environment, if you are adaptable, should hurt your personal progress.

PROBLEM

8

"Who needs other people?"

Molly Backs Away

Although the case does not present Molly's side of the story, the supervisor's interpretation deserves careful consideration. It is quite possible that Molly did not perceive that her unwillingness or inability to communicate freely might have been frustrating to her co-workers who wanted and needed to feel more relaxed around her. They needed a working relationship with Molly that was comfortable even though she may not have felt the same way about it. She may also have failed to recognize that a lack of easy, frequent, and open communication between herself and others increased the possibility of misinterpretation and even prejudice. Two-way communication is absolutely essential for a good, healthy working relationship. *Molly may have been an excellent receiver, but she was apparently a poor sender.*

Whatever Molly's reasons were for remaining rather remote, if she could have seen the need and, if necessary, gained the personal confidence to openly communicate with others, she would have, in all likelihood, been much happier both on and off the job. She had the right to protect her own personal life from those who would have liked to pry, and she had the right to be herself and live her own life style. But she also had an obligation to communicate with others where she worked in the interest of team effort, harmony, and greater productivity.

PROBLEM

9

"Attitude is that important?"

A Challenge for Norman

There was nothing to have kept Norman from looking around for employment with a more youth-oriented company. If things didn't eventually work out well for him, he should have done this. But the indications are that he might have had more of an opportunity to move ahead where he was than he would have had elsewhere. If he moved now, he might be premature. Here's why.

1. Norman might have been letting his limited viewpoint and his older co-workers influence him too much. Just because progress had been slow for many people in the past didn't necessarily mean it would be slow for him; just because some of the older men had lost their positive attitudes didn't mean that Norman had to lose his.

2. The president of the company may have been sincere in wanting to move some aggressive young men into upper echelons, and he may have been doing more about it than Norman thought. Although top management may not have said anything about it, they may have been watching Norman closely and waiting for him to learn enough so they could push him ahead.

3. Three months is a very short period of time in which to fairly evaluate a company and the role you might play in it. Norman should have given the company at least a year, and even then he should have initiated some communication with those upstairs before making a final decision.

From the data presented, it would appear that this organization needed some aggressive young men with fresh approaches and new ideas. Perhaps Norman was hired as an *agent of change*, and if he played the part well there might have been many rewards for him. Perhaps his future was far greater than it appeared on the surface. If Norman accepted the challenge involved in being young and trying to move ahead of more experienced and more mature people—and if he employed sound human relations principles in doing this—then he might have made faster progress than even he suspected. If, however, he let his attitude become negative before he really got started, then he might as well have started seriously looking for a new company. His defeatist attitude could have killed his future before he gave it a chance.

PROBLEM

10

"*Me? Eager?*"

The Eager Beaver

There are many dangers to Ed's approach. How many dangers and how serious they might be would depend on the kind of organization he joined. In some concerns, the tortoise might be more human relations smart than the hare.

The eager beaver often moves so fast that he steps on the feelings of others, thus making human relations mistakes that catch up with him later. He often creates such a dynamic first impression that he cannot sustain it, and he soon becomes known as a flash in the pan. In addition, the eager beaver is not always well organized, and as a result he hurts himself because he lacks the follow-through that establishes good permanent relationships and gets the job done to management's satisfaction.

Ed may have had to learn the hard way that the slower but smoother approach, enabling one to study the ground rules ahead of time, is often the smart way to get started. Too many early mistakes cannot be lived down easily, and steady progress is often the fastest way to the top. It should be said in defense of Ed, however, that there are some highly aggressive and fast moving organizations where his approach would be less dangerous and, in some instances, even desired.

PROBLEM

11

"I put in my eight hours."

Tom's Unexpected Termination

From the limited facts presented, it would seem that Tom was released at the end of the sixty-day probationary period because he did not come through with the management qualities this particular company expected. Apparently the organization was not interested in giving persons who were earmarked for management but who turned out to be average, unmotivated employees permanent status. Therefore they screened them out early. Tom did not quickly demonstrate to the satisfaction of management that he would be a good supervisor. The fact that he was so upset with the decision indicates that he might have taken it for granted that he would receive permanent status by just getting by.

Although most companies would have been more patient and understanding with Tom if he was seriously interested in a management career, he nevertheless should have approached his job with more determination to create a better reputation quickly. He was apparently waiting around for the company to turn him on instead of doing it himself.

PROBLEM

12

"A gal's attitude can stand just so much."

The Difficult Fellow Employee

It is my opinion that Jane did the right thing under the circumstances. After two months she had had sufficient time to discover that the cause of Mrs. Robertson's critical attitude was deep-seated and that time alone would probably not solve the problem. Jane took time to investigate and get some facts. She discovered, among other things, that two former employees in her position resigned because of Mrs. Robertson and her attitude. In other words, this was not surface teasing or testing.

Although it is admitted that Jane took a serious human relations risk by standing up to Mrs. Robertson, she had at least a fair chance of resolving the problem and helping her future. If successful, everybody would come out ahead, including the company and Mrs. Robertson.

The reader may not fully agree with the *way* Jane approached Mrs. Robertson or the way in which she expressed herself. To some it may appear that she was too direct and forceful. To others she may have appeared to be overly apologetic. Everyone must go about confrontations of this nature in his own individual manner. But the principle remains that the cards must often be laid openly on the table if a sound working relationship is to be created or restored.

PROBLEM

13

"As bad as that . . . ?"

Gary's Decision

Gary quickly created an extremely difficult situation for himself. Not only did he foul up his personal reputation as a management trainee among a number of key management people, but he also seriously hurt his horizontal relations with his co-workers. The damage was so serious that Gary might have to look elsewhere for a fresh start.

Although it only took three months to create this situation, restoring or repairing his damaged reputation inside his company could be quite difficult. It takes time to live down a bad reputation. It also takes patience. And in Gary's case, it would take a whole new set of habits. No matter how hard Gary tried, it wouldn't be easy to erase the negative image he had created.

Should he have tried?

It would depend upon whether or not Gary could have found another company that would equal his present one. Could he have located another job as a management trainee in the kind of organization he wanted? Would it have been in the geographical area he wanted? Would it have had all of the advantages and benefits of his present company? If so, it would appear that Gary should have started over. If not, he should have done an about-face and made every effort to wipe out the negative reputation he had foolishly created.

To accomplish this he would have had to do two things: (1) strongly discipline himself as far as being absent or late was concerned, so that no further damage would be done; and (2) make a special effort to rebuild the relationships he previously injured. Neither of these would be easy to do, but Gary's personal progress would depend heavily upon the success he achieved.

PROBLEM

14

"Good listeners are hard to find."

The Poor Listener

Although it is easy to understand the supervisor's impatience with Fay's apparent inability to receive verbal messages, it is doubtful whether his threat to terminate her unless she did an about-face in two weeks was justified. In the first place, Fay was a very sensitive and emotional person, and such an insensitive approach to the problem was bound to cause her to react in a highly emotional manner, thus compounding the problem. In the second place, it would appear that the supervisor should have quietly counseled her once or twice along the way and made a few specific suggestions that might have helped. There seems to be no doubt that the organization could have profited from Fay's talent, so more effort should have been made to resolve the matter.

There are a number of things that Fay could have tried in her attempt to overcome the problem and perhaps save her job: (1) she could have played it safe and gone to a specialist and had her hearing checked; (2) she could have tried to be aware that her mind tended to run ahead of what was being said verbally and, as a result, she didn't get the full message, and that she should concentrate on putting her creative mind out of gear while she was listening to the supervisor's words; (3) she could have tried taking notes while the supervisor was talking to back up the verbal message; (4) she could have asked his permission to bring back preliminary sketches before proceeding; (5) immediately after each verbal communications session, she could have taken some time to think over carefully what had been said before moving ahead with the art work.

PROBLEM

15

"Me? Fall for a rumor?"

Sylvia's Dilemma

Sylvia made two foolish mistakes. First, she accepted as fact a comment that was not authenticated and could easily have been a rumor. Her second mistake, however, was more serious than the first: she permitted the possible rumor to disturb her emotionally to the point where it noticeably hurt her productivity. The facts were not presented in the case, but it is quite possible that the real reason Mr. Young was made department head instead of Sylvia was because her efficiency on the job dropped to the level where management decided to pass her over. If this was what happened, Sylvia permitted a simple rumor to do the greatest possible damage to her future. It is hard to believe that such a sophisticated person could have fallen prey to such an unlikely factor.

PROBLEM

16

"What's in it for me?"

The Preferable Position

Mike had an intriguing but difficult decision ahead of him. In making it he should have taken a deep look at himself.

Where would his personality have fit best? How important was immediate monetary success versus long-range security to him? What were his long-term goals? If Mike became impatient and frustrated over slow but steady progress, he should have thought twice about joining a company with a firm PFW policy. On the other hand, if Mike was willing and could adjust to the longer, slower route, the Metropolitan Company was his best bet. They could provide more and better training, would perhaps encourage him to finish college at night at their expense, and might keep better track of him.

If Mike sought more immediate success, and he was willing to take the risks involved, Great Western would have been his best bet. They might have pushed more responsibility his way sooner; they might also have been less stifling and have expected less conformity. He should have kept in mind, however, that he might have had to train himself more, that the inside competition might have been more aggressive, and that he might not have been given as much time to prepare for additional responsibility. There is also the possibility that he might have found it advisable to move from one company to another to make it to the top. There are many hidden factors involved in such a decision, and Mike should have weighed each one carefully. He would also have been smart to talk it over with his wife, since her happiness was also wrapped up in his decision.

PROBLEM

17

"I'm too good to wait around."

A Danger for Tim

The greatest danger to Tim was that he might lose his positive attitude before he lived through the plateau period and received a substantial promotion. If this happened, chances were good that his productivity would have dropped and his human relations would have suffered. Possible results? (1) The plateau itself might have been extended by management, because with a deterioration of his attitude and productivity they might have decided he was not ready to move up. (2) Tim might have been given a lesser promotion than the one he would have received if he had been able to keep a more positive attitude and wear his patience suit more gracefully. (3) Tim might have been passed over permanently.

Tim needed to be aware of the problem so that he could do everything in his power to protect his positive attitude during this period. If he failed to do this, he might blow the opportunity he had otherwise earned—an opportunity that might have been just around the corner.

PROBLEM

18

"Me and my Big Mouth!"

The Frustrated Engineer

Although Vic's outburst was a natural result of the frustration he felt, it would be difficult to justify it in a man with his education and experience. What could he have done to prevent it? If he somehow could have been sufficiently aware of his building inner tensions, he might have been able to release them harmlessly off the job by working in his yard, playing golf, or taking part in some other physical activity that would better suit his style.

It is doubtful whether Vic had seriously hurt his career at this point. This, of course, depended on the personnel officer who was on the receiving end of the outburst. If he was aware of the frustration-aggression idea, he could have easily appreciated Vic's behavior and not made a negative judgment against him. It is also possible, however, that he could have interpreted the outburst as unstable or immature behavior. To play it safe Vic should have done everything possible to strengthen his relationship with the personnel officer. If he felt an apology was in order, he should have given it.

Vic would have benefited from his experience substantially if it taught him to watch for inner signals of tension so that he could divert any aggressive behavior into harmless channels.

PROBLEM

19

"Better late than never."

A Plan for Lupe

It would appear that Lupe was on a human relations collision course that would result in certain failure unless she reversed her approach in the following two ways. First, she should have stopped flaunting her female charms around in such a way as to encourage hostility from other women. Although she had the right to be relaxed and natural, she would have been smart to play down her wardrobe, body language, and the apparent excessive attention she paid to men on the job. As she did this, she should have concentrated more on building good relationships with the girls by spending more time with them and being more concerned with their problems. Second, she should have set out to prove that she was editorial material by doing superior work in such a way that she would be given opportunities to participate in some of the more exciting assignments. Griping and looking down on her present routine assignments would not accomplish this. Lupe should have helped the editors in such a way that they would go to bat with management to make her an editor.

She might have had to be content to do this bit by bit in a positive and deliberate manner. This wouldn't be asking too much, because she apparently accepted her present job with her eyes wide open.

PROBLEM

20

"Too little . . . too late!"

Too Late with Too Little?

Based on the limited number of facts presented in this case, it would seem that Mark should have seriously considered staying with this company and doing an about-face in human relations. It is never too late to become human relations smart. Mark, if he saw his past mistakes and was serious about his future, had ample time to start building better relationships that could eventually compensate for his earlier mistakes. He should have realized, of course, that this would take a great deal of effort and patience. It wouldn't be easy. Also, he should have been careful not to do a quick about-face and overplay his human relations hand. The reversal should have been a slow, graceful, and positive one.

The one big advantage Mark would have had in starting over with a new company is that he would not have had any mistakes to overcome. His human relations slate would have been clean. However, as long as he had three years invested and liked the company, the personnel policies, and the working conditions, the risk might have been greater in making a change than staying where he was.

Mark should have felt some satisfaction in knowing that it was better to become human relations smart the hard way than not at all.